Y0-CCG-401

RELIGIOUS EDUCATION
IN THE CHURCH

RELIGIOUS EDUCATION
IN THE CHURCH

BY

HENRY FREDERICK COPE

GENERAL SECRETARY OF THE RELIGIOUS EDUCATION ASSOCIATION

NEW YORK
CHARLES SCRIBNER'S SONS
1918

CONTENTS

v

CONTENTS

RELIGIOUS EDUCATION
IN THE CHURCH

CHAPTER I

THE PROBLEM OF ADJUSTMENT

A few years ago there appeared a striking essay entitled "Heckling the Church." It called attention to the fact that every person felt fully qualified to sit in judgment on the church, and to exercise freely his gifts of criticism in this direction. Captious criticism is annoying, but, for the church it is better to be annoyed than to be ignored. If the latter should come to pass the case would be serious indeed. The emphasis of several generations on the primacy of material things has led to the popular assumption that we do not need spiritual institutions. Now we have a renaissance of the spiritual, under the stress of a world agony. But there is a tendency to feel that the spiritual is so implicit in all things that it does not need explicit expression anywhere. Men ask whether a spiritual age needs a special religious institution. Further, various social agencies have taken over many of the activities of the churches. Men are asking whether in the social organization of to-day there remains any special task or place for the church.

These are the questions the present-day church must face. They are not essentially hostile questions. They are expressed by persons of serious minds. They rise within the church rather than without. They are not the questionings of an anti-religious spirit. They come from those with whom religion is taken for granted as a factor in life. The religious institution is not taken for granted. The questions take most serious form under present-day economic pressure. They usually have as a background this inquiry: Precisely where does this special religious institution fit into the scheme of things to-day?

The world is not indifferent to religion; it is becoming more conscious of its spiritual needs. There is almost a religious devotion in the principal charge against the church, that "it is not on to its job." This seems to mean not alone that it is inefficient, but that it does not perceive its task. That is the heart of the problem, the lack of a sufficiently clear, distinct, and definite function, one that will meet a need otherwise unmet, one that will convince the minds, enlist the wills, and win the hearts of all men and women of spiritual perceptions.

The problem of adjustment faces every great social institution. This is the case because society is ever changing in its development, and institutions change and develop also. For instance, the place of the public school is fairly well settled, yet there remain some areas of responsibility in dispute between the school and the family, and, in some countries, large areas in dispute between the schools and the churches.

The problem is intensified for the church, on the one hand, by the fact that this is an age of institutional specialization, and, on the other, by the power of tradition in a religious institution. The age demands that the church accept a clearly defined field and become responsible for this alone. It demands that the task of the church be adjusted to the tasks of other agencies. To do this involves an analysis of responsibilities, a study of the special powers and aptitudes of the church, and a selection of essential tasks. It means change, and change is difficult in proportion to the age and influence of an institution. The church has to struggle against its own institutional crystallization. A host of inherited activities, bound by the ties of tradition and sentiment, so engross the energies, bewilder the mind, and obscure the vision that there are many who are wholly lacking in any clear concepts of the essential nature of the institution, of the work it has to do, and of why it should be done. The result is erratic effort, confused thought, and that uncertainty of mind which undermines conviction, and results in a half-hearted allegiance within and a whole-hearted indifference without.

LEARNING FROM THE CRITICS

Critics rarely acquire the grace of constructive criticism; no one tarries long enough to state what the work of a church really is or ought to be. We are told that the churches fail to relieve poverty; they are helpless before social oppression and injustice; their message is archaic; their methods obsolete; their *métier* gone; they do not preach the gospel; they preach only the gospel; they do not teach politics, amuse the young, teach sex hygiene, solve the trust problem, clean the civic stables, solve international difficulties, or settle the so-called social problem. The things they leave undone are legion. Often the very persons who demand that the church define its social field and maintain the fences thereof are the ones who, when any moral problem perplexes society, turn to the church and say: "You do it."

Perhaps modern criticism, coupled with high expectations, is a compliment to the church as a recognition of her courage and power. It clearly indicates the changed world-conception of the place of the church; she is no longer a "little garden walled around"; she is out in the hurried, tossing stream of human affairs. The question is, whether she has any particular business there. It is frequently assumed that she is incompetent for the great tasks popularly assigned to her.

But popular criticism is careless and often unfair. By what process of reasoning are we justified in blaming the churches because there are thousands of hungry men seeking work in the cities? Might we not, with greater justice, blame the public schools where these men secured life training—such as it was? Or might we not blame the theatre, for instance? True, the theatre has nothing directly to do with the situation, but it has the media for a message, and it withdraws much money which might employ thousands. The point is not that either the theatre or the church is blameworthy or otherwise, but that blame cannot be assigned until responsibilities are determined. We censure hastily because we do not stop to ask, precisely what is the social function of this institution? and we do not seek to determine its social relations and responsibility toward other institutions and toward each of our outstanding modern problems. Even such careless criticism helps, however, by suggesting the need for a careful study of the real task of the church.

We must not forget the criticisms and we can hardly question the sincerity of the large group of ecclesiastical aliens. These men and women are keenly open to spiritual values; they have the vision of the validity and value of the spiritual life; they think of all men as more than machines, and better than eating, talking animals. Many of those who criticise the church because it does not minister to the spiritual needs of men have come to its table and found only dishes, menus, cook-books, and disquisitions on dietetics. They are seriously concerned and deeply disappointed because often in their experiences churches have failed to think of people as persons, and failed in the unique task of stimulating and developing people as religious beings. These critics are essentially religious people, but they are outside of the churches because their very religious life came near to being choked in its dry and dusty clouds of theological argumentation. They found the spiritual dwarfed in an atmosphere of mean and petty striving after offices, social distinctions, and personal advantages, or forgotten in the excitement, the hustling and bustling of bizarre performances.

To these people it seems as though there were two types of churches to-day; the one resembles a monastery into which men retire once a week to hear the mystic phrases of the past, and to consider those things the values of which are determined by their remoteness from life. The other type seems more like a noisy, dusty mill in which a hundred machines are whirling, and a thousand people hustling and shouting, now in the unison and abandon of a common feeling, and now in a pandemonium of conflict called competition; but no one can tell what it is all about, or show that it issues in aught but noise and numbers.

THE STRESS OF READJUSTMENT

The wise man welcomes all honest criticism. He tries to get the critic's point of view. He soothes any pain he may suffer by remembering the words about the wounds of a friend. The critic may be wrong in his conclusions, but he must be right in some of his premises. He bases his judgments on observation. To him it seems that the modern churches are engrossed in a distracting struggle for existence. Many of them appear to be willing to grasp at any straw in the flood, to accept any device for their own preservation. One scheme is tried after another. A nation-wide campaign, which depends for its success on advertising, is adopted to get men into churches. Another campaign is conducted, patterned on the "eat-an-apple" slogan and the "raisin-day" plans, to get people to go to church at least once a year. And then he sees the spectacle of churches outbidding one another for the leadership of "popular preachers" who are sometimes simply spectacular orators. Failing to keep pace with population growth, or even to hold their own by sensational topics for sermons*—all the sensation being usually in the label—or by denatured opera in choirs, they hope to win the world by slang, vaudeville antics, scurrilous abuse, and appeals to prejudice and ignorance. Is this our present-day faith in a gift of tongues— slangy, slanderous, and divorced from knowledge? If this is the dependence of the church, it is surely the last resort, the endeavor of despair.

This is as the critic sees the situation. Perhaps he fails to see that, except for those rare instances where single churches seem to have lost all consciousness of religion, these activities are largely endeavors to discover duties and

* A city in Missouri was plastered with posters announcing as the topic of the sermon at one of the churches, "Hot Stuff for Boys" (1916). Another advertised the topic, "Skidoo, Twenty-three."

secure adjustments in this day of change. They are essays, often crude and short-sighted, toward right relations and adjustments. Whether one approves or condemns, a little thought will enable him to recognize the phenomena of experimentation.

This is a period of adjustment for all social institutions. Just as men specialize more and more exactly in their professions, so society is specializing in its activities. The world does not expect any one institution to be proficient for all the tasks of to-day. It does demand that each one become really proficient in some special task, that it shall be fit to assume responsibility for that task. But who shall make the assignments? No matter how wise this generation may be that question has to be settled largely by social selection, by the survival of the most useful and efficient. The result is that a period of adjustment is a period of struggle. There is much experimentation, some competition, some criticism, and constant adaptation.

SOCIAL CHANGES

That the church is engaged in a struggle for existence no one will question. Modern social life has ceased to take for granted the leadership of the church. The minister is no longer the "parson," pre-eminently the person of the community; the pulpit is no longer the community's intellectual fountain; the church gatherings no longer satisfy popular demands for social intercourse, and allegiance to the church is no longer the indispensable badge of respectability and the gauge of social credit.

Seen objectively, the situation in many communities presents the spectacle of the minister pathetically struggling

to secure influence in community affairs, a small group
endeavoring, by increasing sacrifice and effort, to secure
financial support, the community growing more and more
indifferent, the services of worship attended by decreasing
numbers. We are assured that the situation is the same
everywhere.* Neither the churches that represent religions
of authority nor those that express the authority of religion have the place in the affairs of society that once
they held. But do the empty pews or the losses in direct
political influence tell all the story? Are they sufficient
tests? Applied to the church of a century ago they would
spell failure. To-day they indicate change, change in modes
of influence and power, changes in methods of accomplishing the same purposes. They are symptomatic of adjustment. They may mark the failure of old ways; they indicate the need for new ways. Often the situation rises
out of the attempt to put the new wine of this day's life
and action into yesterday's bottles.

If the conditions briefly characterized above indicate
failure in perfecting adjustments, there are no less striking
evidences of serious efforts to effect proper relationships.
Consider the changes in church edifices from the single room
for worship to the extensive plant providing for classes,
clubs, social life, lectures, recreation, consultation, and
many forms of activity. Consider the changed curricula
of theological seminaries as indicating changes in the minister's professional work. Consider the practical effects of
the movement for social service.† Let the critic study the

* On the situation in England, see chap. II, *The Church and The New
Age*, H. Carter, 1912.

† Consult *A Year Book of the Church and Social Service*, Harry F.
Ward, published by Methodist Book Concern.

organized movement for community betterment in rural districts.* Think of what a really modern church means to a boy or a girl, and compare it with what your church meant to you in boyhood. Think of new methods in Sunday-schools, new educational buildings, curricula, standards, and trained workers. Consider the special organizations for boys and girls. Think of the work of a modern church in relation to recreation as contrasted with its almost single duty as a messenger of warning or denunciation a generation ago. Consider the changes in ideals and methods as to foreign missions. These are but a few of the many changes in the past few decades. They are mentioned not as an inventory of successes, but as indications of endeavors to perfect adjustments. They are symptoms, precisely as significant as the failures and difficulties are.

LOCAL ADJUSTMENTS

One other complicating aspect of the problem of the present-day church must not be overlooked. Not only is the church as a whole in the stress of adjustment to rapidly changing social conditions, but each church is immediately concerned with adjustments to its own local situation. This generation has come to see how different is the ministry of the church in the city from that of the one in the open country, how the suburban type must differ from the downtown type, and how there may be as many different forms of ministry as there are types of communities. It appears that there can be no uniform type even in a single commu-

* For example, see the numerous reports published by the Presbyterian Board of Home Missions; the list will be sent on application to the Board at 156 Fifth Avenue, New York City. See also the publications of the Missionary Education Movement.

nion. Just what any church will do will be determined, first, by the general programme and purpose of all churches, and, secondly, by what needs to be done in that particular community. Manifestly there exist remote and rural communities in which the church will conduct almost every form of social enterprise, or, at least, it will cause them to be conducted. There are also parts of cities where the services of the church will be almost as varied as the needs of the community. There are other parts of the city where the church, surrounded by many efficient agencies, will concentrate on a few forms of service. The wide varieties in local situations make this problem exceedingly intricate. The current attempts at its solution often confuse persons of limited observation. They criticise the city church because it is unlike the country church from which they came. If we are looking for uniformity we are sure to be disappointed in the modern church which seeks efficiency.

If our purpose were that of diagnosing the entire situation as to the churches, it would be necessary to point out in particular the far-reaching effects of economic changes. But, at least, we can keep in mind the general effects by considering the difference between the weekly programme, or routine, of the church-member to-day and the church-member of fifty years ago. The latter was a country— or village—dweller with much leisure; the former is under the pressure of the crowded city, under the strain of a packed programme. When Sunday comes, the modern man has endured about all of the intellectual strain he can stand. He has been in a crowd too long. He needs and longs for rest, for quiet, and, perhaps, for solitude. Even though we recognize the fallacy of the common argument for the golf course as against the church, we must acknowledge that there are very large numbers who must fight inclination, ignore pressing needs, and incur greater nervous strain every time they go to church.

COMPETITION AND DUPLICATION

Frequently our modern efforts to make adjustments to the life of to-day seem to increase our difficulties by bringing the church into competition with other social agencies. Some duplications of activities are unavoidable; some always will exist; some are only a part of the process of discovering duties, but others are without excuse. In the stress of social adjustment the church will have to struggle for her field; it will not be found or held without effort. The church is not the only institution tending to pre-empt more than its share. But it must be confessed that not all the activities of the churches have been designed as serious attempts at social harmony and efficiency.

Many churches are in serious and often bitter competition with other social institutions. Some, as the Roman Catholic Church and certain synods of the Lutheran Churches, attempt the work of public schools, while many of all faiths conduct kindergartens during the week-days. A large number have definite programmes, with elaborate plants, for relief and philanthropic work, covering the ground of charity associations, settlements, hospitals, dispensaries, playgrounds, friendly benefit societies, and other similar agencies. Still others appear to be in active competition with the caterers to public amusement, their services are often degraded to the level of a vaudeville performance in the vain hope of attracting the passing crowd. Sometimes one hears a sermon by a popular preacher which scarcely differs at all from the monologue of the professional comedian. Others conduct week-day programmes of popular entertainments, dramatics, etc., and provide elaborate gymnasiums, playgrounds, restaurants, club-rooms. Others spend energy in organizing forms of secret societies and fraternal lodges. Indeed, scarcely any type of interest develops in modern life but that some church will adopt at least its mechanism in the hope that its attractive power will be maintained when transferred to the church. Here often lies the *raison d'être* of many of these activities; they are adopted as magnets, not as forms of ministry. A church establishes a gymnasium not with the intent of benefiting boys so much as with the hope of "getting hold of the boys." The point of the criticism is not that these enterprises are improper for churches, but that they do not rise out of a clearly apprehended programme; they are extraneous and sporadic efforts to create interest, to get into the game that seems to go on so successfully outside the churches.

THE DEVELOPMENT OF SPECIALIZATION

Frequently there are historic causes for the duplication of activities and the apparent overlapping of fields. Many of the most useful institutions of modern life have developed from the forms of service which the church once rendered. The public schools are the development of the teaching activities of the churches; settlements and charity organizations have grown out of the direct ministry of the church for the poor and the needy; even popular amusements may be traced to the same sources, the miracle-plays, the customs of village dances on the open space before the churches, of games and recreations in the church glebe, and, later, the influence of the "socials" organized by the churches. The splendid activities of the Young Men's Christian Associations and the Young Women's Christian Associations are the fruitage of the sincere efforts of churches to meet the physical, mental, and spiritual needs of youth. We can never afford to lose sight of the fact which history so patently records that the church has been the mother of almost all those forms of social service with which her work is to-day so often unfavorably contrasted.

But it is a part of the function of all worthy institutions to give birth to agencies which will ultimately deprive them of phases of their earlier activities. It is an evidence of efficiency when an institution conducts so well one form of service that part of its organization develops into self-support and autonomy. The church ought not to talk about competition with social settlements, or with the Y. M. C. A.; it ought rather to be grateful that it has children grown to such stature and so efficient as to bring high credit on their parentage. However, the pertinent question arises, When the offspring take over all the duties and divide all the field among themselves, what remains to the parent institution? What, to-day, is the place of the church in the social order?

THE TESTING TIME

Have we come to a time when, because the earlier activities of the churches are now more efficiently carried on by other agencies, the church can pass properly out of existence, a rich historic memory, but no more? That is much more than a philosophical question. Many return an affirmative answer. Many thousands, who have never given the matter any historical study, assert most emphatically that the "church has outworn its time of service," "outgrown its usefulness," "is a vestige only of the past." These all listen with indifference to the call of the churches; they meet its appeals for support with the charge of inefficiency and economic waste. Some are simply guilty of the very bigotry they usually denounce; but besides these there are serious-minded persons who are asking what right the churches have to the investment which society is asked to make in them.

In an increasing degree the economic test will be applied. The churches will be judged by the economic return they make to society for the investment made in them. The test is neither unfair nor illogical. Here is an institution which holds immensely valuable real estate, some of the best sites in a city, which asks for support in large sums, which withdraws from other occupations many professional workers and makes large drafts on the energies of many thousands of persons. With all this financial, personal, and temporal investment, what are the returns? On what grounds do we justify the investment? Is it simply in order that groups of people here and there shall continue to do in an amateur manner that which other agencies are doing with professional expertness? Is all this cost of life only that churches shall be supported to play at instruction, relief, social amusement, and recreation? Some aim, distinct, clearly apprehended, and commanding, will need to emerge, or society will not long justify the investment it is asked to make.

All this does not mean that we must immediately give up the old ship, saying that her cargo has been transferred to a flotilla of new craft. But it does mean that there must be a square facing of the question as to the precise function of the church in our day. She must cease to carry on traditional activities without regard to whether they are better done elsewhere or are needed at all; she must cease the attempt at winning popular support by a round of factitious activities; she must cease the attempt to manufacture convincing programmes without consideration of the value of the performances.

The Jack of all trades is out of date. The barber who was also surgeon, physician, chiropodist, and nurse is no more. The teacher who taught all subjects now teaches none. The general merchant remains only in remote districts. Life is specialized. There is no longer need for the church to generalize in all good things, for there are other agencies and institutions much more efficient in some good things. She must specialize, must deliberately discover what is her specialty and then stick to it.

REFERENCES

CARTER, H., *The Church and the New Age* (Hodder & Stoughton, 1912).
STRAYER, P. M., *The Reconstruction of the Church* (Macmillan, 1915).
CROOKER, J. H., *The Church of Tomorrow* (Pilgrim Press, 1911).
MATHEWS, S., *The Church and the Changing Order* (Macmillan, 1907).

CHAPTER II

WHAT IS THE FUNCTION OF THE CHURCH?

EFFICIENCY depends on the answer. The grave criticism of the church is not that she is doing so little, but that she is trying to do so many things, and doing few or none of them well. Perhaps it would be more exact to say that the church is attempting more duties than any single institution can discharge and often without a clear understanding of why many of them should be attempted. She lacks the clear consciousness of field and task which would indicate duties exactly.

We cannot answer the question as to function until we know the nature of a church. What is a church, not only historically but objectively as we see it to-day? One does not need to depend wholly on the genesis and history of the church in order to determine its task in the life of to-day. It may well be that the church of the first century had a function quite different from that of the modern church. The church at Ephesus, partially isolated, facing a heathen world ignorant of its philosophy and faith, would take up tasks wholly different from those facing the rich, powerful church in New York or London. The church in Foochow would have waiting opportunities different from either Ephesus or London. The church in Hornby, N. Y., will face rural situations differing widely from those of the scattered congregations of the first century. But, after all, there is an unvarying underlying principle for all, and all have certain common characteristics. No matter how

churches may differ, each one is a group of people agreed
on placing the religious values first in life.* Wherever a
church may be, whatever its policy and its creed, it is a
society united by the concept of the Godlike possibilities of
man. A church is a group of persons associated and co-
operating for the sake of personal, or spiritual, values. This
does not precisely define a Christian Church; it is only a
statement of its central ideal in simple, inclusive terms.

Now a church exists, not because there are programmes
for its social activity, but, first of all, because people always
will get together. The social instinct polarizes human beings, and it is most likely to draw them about the poles of
their ideals. Given a sufficiently attractive personal and
social ideal, the get-together instinct, or habit, will bring
people around the ideal. That is what happens whenever
a church is formed. In the Christian religion the ideals
are essentially personal and social; the church is a group of
persons polarized at the personal ideal of Jesus and the
social ideals he taught. The most satisfying thing that can
happen to any of us is to come along with others to a common consciousness of such commanding, elevating ideals.
This is the basic justification of a church. The social unity
of the Christian Church in the consciousness of the leadership of Christ and the endeavor to realize his character
and ideal are values immeasurable and essential to all
permanent human progress.

THE PERSONAL CLEW

A church consists of persons; its processes deal with
persons; its product is personal. It is a social institution

* See George A. Coe in *Psychology of Religion*, chap. VIII.

because it is a personal institution in the plural, and wherever you have real personality in the plural you have society. In the last analysis, when we have worked down through ritual, ordinances, services, creeds, and forms of activity, when we can see these as means and processes, the end and the product clearly appear as *people*. All seek a personal and, therefore, a social product.

The church exists to deal with persons, as religious persons, to the end that they may find in themselves, and as a social whole, fulness of life; as one has said, that men might become like God and this earth like heaven; as the apostles put it, that men might be saved, that the world might be saved; and as Jesus put it, that men might have life and that they might have it more abundantly. Here is the ultimate purpose of the church: Godlike men and women in a world of God's will. Here is the programme of the church: To reach all men in all their lives to the end that this purpose may be realized. Here is the process of the church with men: Developing in them this Godlike life according to the laws of that life.

Such a statement as this may seem to be very elementary, yet in how many instances would the application of the principle—that the church exists for the sake of people—work a complete revolution in church methods! The principle in its simplicity needs to be stated frequently. By it we may test every enterprise and activity in the church. It puts life at the centre. It sets in present-day terms Jesus' teaching on the primary place of personal values. It helps to clarify the message of the church on modern world-problems by the example of an institution definitely and consciously devoted to the democratic task of developing people. It thus not only insists that a man is worth more than a sheep, but that he is worth more than constitutions and institutions.

The importance of such simple considerations appears when we realize that a clear view of the task is necessary in order to discover the function of the church. To apprehend the function and to make it clear to men will settle such outstanding questions as whether the church has a justifiable place in the modern world, and whether there remains to the church a clear, comprehensible, practical task in the life of to-day.

But does loyalty to a personal, religious ideal demand the intricate organization and elaborate mechanization of the churches of to-day? A partial answer to the question is that loyalty to such a personal ideal demands efficient, persistent endeavor to secure its commanding place in all lives and through all social relations. The church is a group of persons associated at the point of a personal ideal so lofty in character as to compel them to make it known to all, equally potent to all, and regnant through all human affairs. This group accepts the character and authority of their leader; the ideal commands their lives. Loyalty means not simply admiration, nor imitation, it means that which is the essential spirit of the Christian Church, the dominating desire, the compelling passion that all men shall know this ideal, shall become like their leader, and shall rejoice to do his will. So this little social group, gathered about an ideal, becomes a body with a propaganda: to lead all men to the likeness of their leader, to make all men in character like him and to make this world the place where his will is done.

It is the only institution which includes all the members of the social group in this one spiritual purpose. It is the only voluntary agency with the specific purpose of interpreting life as spiritual growth.* It is the only one which regards persons primarily as religious beings. It is the only one which, dealing with both men and women, with young and old, definitely sets character first and deliberately seeks to realize in them the highest known ideal of character. It is the only complete social group with the function of developing human character toward divine perfection.

COMPLICATING FACTORS

If the task of the church is so simple, clear, and definite, how does it happen that she has so often lost sight of it? Why have so many other aims become dominant at various times? Why is the picture of the work of the church vague and confused in the minds of so many of her people? It is in part because, while the personal aim is very simple, the method of realizing it is always exceedingly complex. In the past, as the church pursued her task, she found that the growth of character was a multiplex process. Not only did it have to do with ideals presented through teaching, preaching, and worship, but it depended on health, physical environment, and forms of activity. The growth of character was the growth of the whole of personality. Its programme

---

* One wonders whether to add: "except the Young Men's Christian Association, the Young Women's Christian Association, and, perhaps, other similar organizations." But the fact is we cannot think of them apart from the churches. They would scarcely claim a complete institutional independence. Moreover, they deal only with certain groups. A good case may be made for the family as ideally an institution primarily for religious purposes; but society is not generally conscious of such an interpretation.

demanded the domination of all social relations by the religious ideal. General education, hospitals, social relief, civic improvement, all grew out of the endeavor of the church to furnish a soil in which lives might grow up and move forward. The stimuli of the Godward and Godlike life came out of the entire environment.

Character is growing all the time. What a person will be is being determined on the street as well as in the church. Every-day environment may be just as potent as Sunday environment. The religious purpose of the church cannot be accomplished by dealing with souls which come out of seclusion only for sacred services. These souls are in the world. The world-conditions must be made to co-operate with the work of the church. To carry forward her programme the church must cause conditions to prevail in society which are favorable to spiritual ends.

When the churches began relief work they took up the neglected task of laying sound physical foundations for a good life. When the modern church engages in social reform her aim, ideally, is the control of the conditions which help to determine character. So deeply is the life of the spiritual being set in the soil of every-day living that he cannot even will his growth toward high ideals save as that soil helps this growth.

THE MENACE OF MACHINERY

Why have we so often lost sight of the commanding and inspiring aim of personal and social development? Is it not largely because of the complexity of the process? This is a large programme, to control social life and make it favorable to spiritual ends. The effort to develop the necessary

machinery and to secure sufficient resources absorbed the
energies of leaders. Attention was concentrated on the
means. The church became less an instrument of ministry
and more an institution to be ministered to, and the important issue then became that of preserving the church,
and thus its ministry to society was converted into an effort
to maintain the agency. In the same manner men often
became more anxious about the doctrine than about its
effect on character. They substituted the means for the
end, the tools for the product. They so sedulously guarded
the tools, that is, the doctrines, creed, organization, and
ordinances, that they forgot altogether that these only
had value as they served the high purposes of making men
more like the ideal One, and society more like that which
he pictured. Indeed, the tools and means have vitality
only as long as they serve worthy and adequate purposes.

It is always easy for the machine, being the object of immediate attention, to seem to be of greater importance than
the product. This is not strange, for the institution, the
machine, is so obvious, so necessary, and so engrossing. It
is a definite thing for which one can work. But it becomes
a dangerous thing when it becomes an end in itself. We
have constantly to face the peril of forgetting the great
end in the lives of persons. Organization, property, and
officials must be held subservient to the interests of the
people who are to be saved. Few dangers are more insidious
than that we shall think that the churches exist for the
sake of preaching, music, forms of worship, statements of
belief, types of service, membership rolls, magnificent buildings. The personal aim must dominate and we must
insist that all these are but tools and processes for specific

personal ends, valuable only as they minister to these ends.
The church does not exist in order to preach the gospel,
but the church preaches the gospel in order that men may
exist as religious beings, that they may know their heavenly
Father, love him, and be like him.

Facing the problem of maintaining the means of adjusting social conditions to spiritual ends, the church must not
forget that the personal programme is the most effective
one.   People determine conditions even more than conditions
determine people. Social conditions, ultimately, are not
determined by compulsion, legislation, or regulation; they
are determined by the ideals and wills of men and women.
The kingdom of heaven rises within.   As a wise teacher said:
"The soul of all improvement is the improvement of the
soul."   Loyalty to the task of leading lives into spiritual fulness is the way out of the difficulty for the church.   Then
these lives, as they develop, reach out and dominate social
conditions; they will a right world. Therefore, the church
needs often to emphasize the personal and spiritual aim.   In
a world where the material and external so strongly appeal
she must insist on the eternal, the personal. Regardless of
other agencies, her prime and directing duty lies with people
as people.

The special need of the church at this moment is an
examination of her activities, an evaluation of them by this
test, Do they serve the function of the church in the direct
development of Christian character and the organization of
a society of good-will? If the church exists to develop
Christian character and to cause Christian conditions to
prevail in human society, how far is her machinery adapted
to that end, and what are the best methods to follow?

There exists already a test of all her work—the kind of people that she gives to society.

Another important question remains to be asked, Can the work of spiritual development be most efficiently maintained at present by this institution, or is it being carried on better by others?

That question cannot be answered empirically. It rests on another and very fundamental one, What are the methods by which the aim of the church is to be realized? In the flood of light which modern science begins to throw on the processes of human development, what do we find to be the means by which personality develops, character grows, and the social whole is brought along the way to its spiritual ideal? When we have discovered these laws we shall be able to determine the type of social institution best fitted to work under them. Of this we can be certain: it will be a social institution, a group of persons, and it will be controlled by great and compelling spiritual ideals. Whether it be new or old it will have the organic elements which characterize the churches to-day. Even if the churches as now constituted should cease to exist, other social organizations would spring into existence to carry on this work and in all essentials they would find themselves very soon so like the churches as not to be distinguishable from them. In many incidental and external features they would differ, but they would still be groups gathered about commanding personal ideals. They would still be devoted to spiritual ends. They would still find it possible to do their work only by methods indicated by the laws of lives. They would still find their work possible only under the motive of a self-giving passion for lives.

Perhaps it were well to stop and ask whether the function of the development of religious character is so clear, so outstanding, so differentiated, and so simple as to constitute a sufficient reason for the existence of this special institution? The answer would be that whether or not there is any general appreciation of the need of special training in religious character the obligation remains just as strong on all who have seen its need and caught its glory. But already modern society does recognize the fundamental place of the personal equation; it is consciously built on the basis of character and increasingly it tends to interpret life in the religious terms of service and sacrifice, and consequently, society will justify the work of the churches.

PRACTICAL PLACE

The function of the church is just as clear as the function of a system of transportation, just as definite as the function of a public school, just as real as the function of a manufacturing plant, and, at least, fully as necessary as any. The so-called practical man may object, saying that you can weigh, count, and measure the goods with which the factory deals while the spiritual aims of the church are altogether vague and elusive. The man who talks in that strain should know that even in the manufacture of the most prosaic goods there enter elements that cannot be weighed or counted, that cannot even be bought or sold. He knows that the character and ambitions of workmen, the temperaments of salesmen, the psychology of advertising, the general tone of business confidence, and the factor of business faith and credibility all enter into the making and marketing of his goods. If he does not think often of the values of these factors he is not an efficient manufacturer. If he knows nothing of them he is blind to the largest facts in life. He is a man working with one eye, the thing-seeing eye, and without the eye that sees thought, emotions, judgments, character, and will.

We have to recognize the existence of the one-eyed man, but we confess to a conviction that the affliction is voluntary, though of so long standing as to seem incurable. All spiritual, idealistic movements appear to this man to offer an easy excuse when he is urged to support them; he says they are vague and visionary. If he could see their value he would support them, and therefore he cannot see their value.

Is it not possible, with these general considerations of the specific task of the church to-day, to state its function in precise terms? It has to do with persons; it exists to develop them toward certain personal and social ideals. Its functions, therefore, belong in the same group with other agencies organized for the direction and stimulation of personal development, particularly with the schools. In other words, it is engaged in education, in developing lives. *The social function of the church is that of education, and particularly moral and religious education.*

Before this statement of function can be accepted fully it may be necessary to see just what the modern concept of education involves, and, also, whether it really includes and properly defines the specific work which the church can undertake in the life of to-day.

REFERENCES

GLADDEN, WASHINGTON, *The Church and Modern Life* (Houghton Mifflin, 1908).

CROOKER, J. H., *The Church of Tomorrow*, chap. II (Pilgrim Press, 1911).

STRAYER, P. M., *The Reconstruction of the Church*, part II, chap. I (Macmillan, 1915).

CARTER, H., *The Church and the New Age*, sec. 3, chap. I (Hodder & Stoughton, 1912).

VOTAW, C. W., and ST. JOHN, EDWARD P., *The Church in Moral and Religious Education*, papers in *Religious Education*, December, 1909, pp. 410–423 (Religious Education Association).

CHAPTER III

WHAT DO WE MEAN BY EDUCATION?

HAVING defined the function of the church as an educational one, it is necessary to inquire, What do we mean by education? It would be too large a task to attempt a complete and detailed definition of the meaning of education; but it is necessary to agree upon a general working statement. This is not easy because the meaning is changing and enlarging rapidly to-day. To superficial minds education means simply the process of instruction carried on in schools and colleges. To such persons education begins at about six or seven years of age, when the child leaves the shelter of the family; it may continue up to fourteen, eighteen, twenty-one, or twenty-two; it ends when he leaves school. Schooling and education are regarded as synonymous. The phrase "finished his education" is still current; it simply means that the period of formal schooling is ended. Unfortunately, it too often expresses the more significant fact that directed development also has ceased. We need to exercise greater precision in the uses of "schooling" and "education." We still share too generally the opinion of the young college graduate who, on receiving his bachelor's diploma, is said to have telegraphed to his parents the laconic message: "Educated."

A PERSONAL PROCESS

Modern education is a *personal process*. In its essential sense education means the orderly development of persons,

according to the laws of personal growth, into the fulness
of their powers, into the efficiencies, habits, joys, and values
of their lives and their world. It is based upon confidence
that human beings are capable of development. It holds
that the process of personal growth is not completed by
nature, but must be stimulated and directed. It holds that
man's growth is not of body alone, but is of the whole person.
It believes that this process of personal development is
continuous with the whole of life. It insists that it is the
duty of society to direct this process and enrich its results.

Modern education emphasizes the fact that it deals with
persons, not with minds or memories or hands alone. It
seeks to develop that being of nerves, feeling, will, judgment,
and conduct called a person. It is concerned with what one
has illuminatingly called "behaving organisms." * It awak-
ens, stimulates, and trains the powers of a life. It directs
abilities and develops control of will and conduct. Its
methods are based upon our knowledge of the processes of
feeling, knowing, willing, and doing. They are determined
by the way in which a person knows, judges, discerns,
values, feels pleasures and pains, determines conduct, and
carries feeling and will into action. Education is not concerned alone with storing the memory with facts, or filling
the mind with so-called mental equipment. These are
but means like food or tools. It is concerned with securing
the development of persons who will fit into, live fully with,
and serve, their world of persons.

* See William James in *Talks on Psychology and Life's Ideals*, chap.
III (Henry Holt, 1906). This is apparently the underlying concept
in W. C. Bagley's valuable *Educational Values* (Macmillan, 1911).
For a summary of many definitions of education, see pp. 85–90 of
Principles of Education, C. Ruedeger (Houghton Mifflin, 1910).

A SOCIAL PROCESS

Thinking thus of developing persons, modern education becomes essentially a *social process*, for the persons with whom it works do not live alone, they think and feel and do in a world of other persons. What life is to them is determined by this world of persons. They, too, help to determine the world for other persons.* Modern education is essentially social rather than individual. It is not thinking merely of the quiet, dignified, scholarly gentleman sitting in refined seclusion in his book-lined study. It has in mind our whole social life. The growth of persons is stimulated and modified by the fact that we tend increasingly to the polarization of life. We live in crowds and have to learn not alone to live in society, but to live the life of the social whole.

MORAL IMPLICATIONS

Modern education is, therefore, because it deals with beings whose very life is social and who are living in the social whole, essentially a *moral process*. This is involved in any clear picture of education as the development of active persons learning to live in society, for morality is wholly a matter of social living. Morality begins at the point at which my neighbor's life touches mine. Out of those relations rise all moral situations. Whatever moral conduct a man living on a desert island might have would either grow out of past social relationships or be directed to possible future relationships. This would be true, also, as to the ideal relationships in the conscious reality and

* See John Dewey, *School and Society* (Univ. of Chicago Press), and particularly W. C. Bagley in *The Educative Process*, chap. III.

nearness of friends who continue to live in memory and in spiritual life real in his own consciousness.

When we talk about teaching morality in schools we usually mean teaching ethics, that is, the formalized rules of conduct determined by the accumulated experience of a society. But morality goes much deeper than that. It is more than the rules of conduct. It underlies all rules because it is a mode or manner of life which arises out of the fact that we live in social relations so close that all we do becomes a part of other lives. My life is set in the midst of many other lives and is never out of relation to them, so that what life means, and what I shall be and do, is determined by this fact. The word morality has its root in the *mores*, the customs of the tribe; but what does that mean other than the principles which have developed in the making of the tribe, its organization, adjustment, and unification into a social whole? Morality is the art of living as conditioned by the fact of a world of persons. Moral living is simply living in the full light of other lives, in loyalty to their needs and rights. If education is social it must be essentially moral. Moral living is implied in all learning; even in the formal curriculum the subjects of study have value and meaning because of their power in guiding conduct under social relations. We cannot avoid the moral interpretation of education.

THE WIDER MORAL UNIVERSE

But if we consider further the moral significance and aim of education it will open up yet larger meanings. The social relationships of a person reach out further than friend and neighbor; they go out to all persons who can possibly come into the realm of consciousness. Our neighboring must go out as far as thought and consciousness can go. It evidently has no geographical bounds. Neither has it any physical bounds. The memory of the dead influences conduct and determines ideals. The great souls of all the yesterdays continue to live in the most vital and influential social relationships with all thinking beings to-day. Here is no small element in the real enriching of life and the world through education. The ignorant man is he of the circumscribed world; he knows not at all the great procession of souls who have gone on before and who still stand about all who seek fellowship with them. Socrates, Jesus, Amos, Homer, Euripides, Dante, and the innumerable host are in our social world and help to make us what we are. They are near to us because their spirit has been treasured in deathless words and ideals. In the unfading power of such spirits we recognize the deathless spirit of man. So also, according to the reality of our living, does the selfhood of each of us go down through the ages. In like manner all ages become ours, mediated to us through the spirits that cannot die. Thus, in part, we find ourselves in a spiritual universe. The world of spirits is our society, also.

Nor is this wider reach of social relationships confined to the great souls that shine through the misty past. In no uncertain way do others, unknown to fame, live with us. Our world of personality includes many souls. Friends die, but friendship, the social essential, remains. Underneath all these finite relationships, and expressing itself in them, is the "love divine all love excelling." Each one knows that in such relationships, in the fact that there are other lives which one may really know, lies one of the elements

of the unchanging value and reality of life. Education deals
with persons capable of such relationships, persons whose
life reaches out to all life, who live in the spirit because they
are spirits. Education deals with persons who are body,
mind, feeling, and will, whose lives are personal, lived in a
world of personal, and, therefore, spiritual relationships.
Education is a *spiritual* process.

THE AIM OF EDUCATION

One other consideration must be mentioned briefly. If
education is the directed development of such a person, in a
world that embraces all time and all being, it deals with
him for *the purpose of developing his entire powers*. It seeks
to make him efficient to live, that is, to cause knowledge,
feeling, and judgment to issue in right conduct. Now
conduct wherever it is voluntary is largely determined by
motives. A motive is the sum of one's judgment and feeling
as to the meaning and values in a situation. It is the sense
of duty or of desire which indorses or prohibits an action.
Innumerable elements enter into a decision to act even
though it is made in a lightning-flash. These elements have
been accumulating over a long time by the way we have
learned to look at things, to choose one kind of good or
another. An interpretation of life enters into and guides,
more or less consciously, every deliberate act. By the development of habits and by the formation of judgments on
life's values, all conduct is being continuously determined.
Habit is the mechanism and motive is the mainspring of the
moral life, the life of intelligent, responsible, social conduct.
What life is to you as you see it in all its breadth, what its
possibilities are to you, what it means of fellowship and of

joy, these are its values. These meanings make every motive. These meanings are your religion. The judgment values, the meaning and interpretation of life constitute the essential, vital, distinguishing element in each person's religion.* Without this element education is helpless in its programme of developing persons into fulness of social living. It must reach the controls of conduct and, therefore, it comes back to life's interpretative ideals—to religion. In this sense all persons are essentially religious; they cannot be satisfied with the immediate phenomena of life, but they must search out its meaning, and especially its meaning for them. And since they are guided in life by the meaning they discover, education must recognize that it deals with religious beings and constantly must take this essential fact into account.

THE RELIGIOUS QUALITY

Does not this suggest that education, dealing with spiritual beings, cannot escape religious significance? It may speak of its processes as though they were limited to realms outside of religion, but the truth is, that it cannot develop a person in parts or fractions of his life; it must reach and grow all the man, and, therefore, must deal with him as a spirit, as a religious being. It is determining the size of his universe, the value of his ideals, and the habits of his life. But all the time it has to do with one whose essential life is in the spirit, in the realities of values, meanings, relationships, and possibilities that can be comprehended and explained in no terms short of a spiritual society.

* See George A. Coe's statement for this "revaluation of values" on pp. 68–70 in *Psychology of Religion* (Univ. of Chicago Press, 1916).

There is, then, a sense in which all education is religious education because it deals with persons who are in nature religious. It deals with them for ultimately religious purposes, that they may live in a world of spiritual beings. It is also true that, in a sense, its processes are religious, since they are only scientific so far as they are based on the unchanging laws of the universe as discovered in the natures of these spiritual beings. This concept of education we need to foster. In all teachers, in ourselves, we need to develop the sense of dealing with religious persons, of being always engaged in religious work.

There is an important sense in which all formal education is religious, since it directs itself specifically to deal with spiritual beings and cannot escape that relationship and responsibility. But it is very important, for the sake of definiteness in thinking, to consider education in its precise methods, in its directed, determinative forms. Among these methods and forms, we must consider those in which the concept of religious persons and the purpose of preparing them for religious living in a religious society rises definitely into consciousness. If the religious quality of education and its spiritual aim are to be clearly maintained then religion must be explicit as well as implicit.

To say that all education is religious is only, after all, to say that all life is religious. But in order that life may be religious, men and women must know what are the religious qualities and values in life. They must know in what manner and by what means men have given expression to the religious interpretation of life. The life of the spirit must have its own food, its light and nurture. True, it feeds on all forms; but all forms become its food only as they are clearly seen in relationships to life's wider, spiritual meanings and powers. Such relationships must be made clear; they must be revealed and explained. If religion is this life as determined in its meanings by the high consciousness or hope of social relationships with the widest, furthest reach of being,* of the spirit of man with all spiritual life, and with God the father of spirits, then this wider, furthest circle of life must be apprehended that its existence may interpret all our present life. It must be known and understood in order that it may give value, meaning, and direction to all experience. Moreover, each life needs the enriching of its heritage in all that the race has accumulated of such ideals. It needs the light and guidance of the experience of all past lives. It needs the impulse, the motives that come from all that the religious spirit has known and felt and achieved.

Education then is the directed development of persons into the full experience of all their social universe. Specifically, religious education is training and instruction in the life of the larger, infinite spiritual society. It is the education of a religious person by religious means, for religious living in a religious social order which is part of a spiritual universe. It is training man as the child of God for the family of God.

* See Prof. G. A. Coe's treatment of religion as the discovery of persons and society in chap. XIV of *The Psychology of Religion*.

REFERENCES 37

REFERENCES

J., *What Do We Mean by Education?* (Macmillan, 1915).
BAGLEY, W. C., *The Educative Process* (Macmillan, 1905).
MOORE, ERNEST C., *What is Education?* (Ginn & Co., 1915).

II. RELIGIOUS EDUCATION

COE, GEORGE ALBERT, *A Social Theory of Religious Education* (Scribners, 1917).
KING, HENRY C., *Personal and Ideal Elements in Education* (Macmillan).
RELIGIOUS EDUCATION ASSOCIATION, *The Bible in Practical Life* (Convention papers, 1904).
Religious Education, the bimonthly magazine of the Religious Education Association, contains many articles on both the principles and the methods of religious education.

CHAPTER IV

THE MEANING OF EDUCATION IN THE CHURCH

The difficulty of thinking of the church as "an educational agency" lies in the fixed meaning we have attached to the adjective. Speak the word "education," and there flashes before the mind a picture either of college buildings set about a campus or of a classroom containing a teacher and learners. Popularly, an educator is one who, being possessed of a large quantity of information, is employed to distribute that information to less fortunate—but not at all envious—young persons.

Popular views are often misleading. Many persons suspect that "education" is simply a high-sounding phrase for the simple art of clothing the naturally naked mind with the garments of information. The information-acquisition idea is still prevalent. Here is the teacher, a peripatetic warehouse of facts; here is the child or youth, comparable to an empty freight-car; here is the machinery of the schoolhouse, tracks to switch the car up to the warehouse, mechanisms to hold the car during the loading process, authority to determine when the car is duly loaded, and to place an official seal or tag certifying to the same. Popularly, the educated man has been through this process; the man who has taken any other process is not educated; a college degree is the way-bill of this freight-car routing it to social and business success, though by no means insuring delivery.

Such general conceptions are emphasized because from them principally arises the difficulty of accepting an educational definition of the function of the church. To say that the church is an educator is to suggest a picture of the church organized for purposes of instruction, its buildings converted into academic halls, its leaders wearing college gowns, and its people, young and old, meekly seated in classes, while its product for the world is a freightage of information about religious history, literature, and philosophy. Because we all know that converting a church into a theological seminary would not make it a more religious institution, and certainly would not meet the real and deep needs of the human group about it, we reject that concept of its mission.

But the acceptance of the educational function of the church does not at all involve its conversion into an academic institution. It does not mean that its chief workers shall be learned persons spiritually dying from undigested information. It does not mean converting the sermon into a lecture, and every meeting into a class. It does not mean substituting thinking for being, definitions for deeds, glorifying knowledge as an end in itself, and substituting parchments and participles for people.

It is true that a few churches, emphasizing the word education in large type on their bulletins, and boasting of curricula arranged to resemble college catalogues, have tried to woo the world by the fascination of academic terminology. They have thought they were educational institutions because they had systems for imparting information which would insure that if they could have a child from primary to graduate years he would know as much as a whole faculty of theology. Such programmes have been born in a fever of intellectual pride and died in the frost of human indifference.

THE SOCIAL PROCESS IN THE CHURCH

But, for the church as for us all, education means a whole life process in which knowledge plays an important, but essentially subsidiary part. The educational programme in the church means, first, that she is organized as a social institution which accepts *the purpose of developing persons* to the fulness of their lives as its prime responsibility. The special function of the church grows out of her recognition of persons as religious beings and her loyalty to the purpose to develop in them the fulness of life as religious persons. The educational programme simply means that whatever the church does, in all things, is determined by the one controlling purpose to bring men toward God in character, likeness, and conscious relationships. The church is an educator in the degree that, because of her existence and work, men actually do grow in the spiritual life, the kind of life that is spiritual in character and reach, and in the degree that society comes nearer to the will of God in the spiritual interpretation of all life.

A family is an educational agency in the degree that all its life, its organization, its activities, and relationships are determined by its purpose to inspire, stimulate and direct those lives for which it is responsible.

There are workshops that are truly educational agencies. They stimulate, inspire, and develop lives. People come out of them knowing and feeling more fully what life means, and being more competent to live.* But with the church, the maintenance of such processes is her sole aim and function.

True educational programmes go far beyond all mechanisms for imparting information. Telling folks things or tethering them to text-books is not the distinguishing feature of an educational church. Whatever is directed to developing, enriching, co-ordinating, and controlling the powers of a life is education. The classroom is but a small part of that programme.

There is danger, too, of similar misunderstanding when we seek to define more exactly the purpose of the church and speak of its programme as one of religious education. That danger lies in the error of thinking of religious education as a matter of acquiring knowledge about religion. We use the word "religion" as defining the quality and aim of the process, not alone as defining the content of any body of teaching. Religious education in the church simply means the organization of those methods and processes which develop persons as religious beings into efficiency in living in a religious society.

THE EDUCATOR'S FAITH

The educational programme is based, second, upon *faith in life as growth*. Religious education regards persons as having the capacity or possibility of growth in powers, in personality, and in the whole range of life. The first article of its creed is that man was made to grow, and it extends

* See "Character Development Through Social Living," H. F. Cope, *Religious Education*, vol. IV, pp. 401–410.

this article by the faith that man was made to grow to the utmost fulness of being of which man has conceived. We cannot but believe that if man can think of God, man must go on to be in character like that of which he thinks. The aim is no less than men growing into the likeness of the Most High. That which distinguishes religious education from general education is the explicit recognition of the greater range of powers in the person being educated. It regards the child, not simply as having a mind, nor alone as a potential citizen, housekeeper, and wage-earner; it regards him as possessed of Godlike qualities, as destined to larger life in a society which holds in one life God and all mankind. To religious education he is more than an intelligence to be developed, he is a person to come to the fulness of life in a universe explicable only on the basis of the supremacy of personality.

Religious education to-day stands as a vital, inspiring faith in the world. It is rich in spiritual aspiration. It is faith in growth. It is faith in the possibilities of human life. Faith in the processes of education marks the difference between the human family and the bird-nest. This faith accounts for the school. Both stand to say to us all: We believe in life; we believe that man was made to grow and not to stop. The advance of the race is marked by the measure of this faith. You may know where any people are by the length of time they give children in which to grow, and by the adequacy of the provisions they make for the direction and stimulation of their growth. Children at eight, under primitive conditions, could shift for themselves; but we prolong infancy, we extend it to, perhaps, twenty or more, because we count it possible to spend all those years in real growth. We count life so large a thing that it tends to require longer periods of preparation. All this means at root a faith in the worth of life.

Moreover, religious education aims at a religious ideal; not only that the person shall find himself fulfilled in the divine likeness, but that all persons shall find life in the religious ideal of a divine society. It seeks to develop people for living in a social whole which shall be like the family of God. It therefore does not deal alone with individuals, it deals with the movement of a common life called society.

Does some one say, all these views the church has long held regarding people, these interpretations of the meaning of personality are her special contribution? True, as views they have long been held, but have they been acted upon? To what extent have churches accepted the consequences of their own views of the meaning of life? Holding that men were the children of God, what programmes have been adopted for growing men into the family likeness? What evidence is there that we have expected that this likeness would ever be a reality, or anything more than a dim, poetic ideal? We have accepted the destiny of man without ever hoping it would be realized in this world at all, or, if we have hoped for its realization, we have failed to inquire as to means and processes thereto.*

A CALL FOR A PROGRAMME

The acceptance of the educational purpose—the growth of Godlike lives in a society of the God-will—lays upon the

* On this general failure in education see *Social Environment and Moral Progress*, A. R. Wallace, 1913.

church the duty of discovering an educational programme. It involves the study of all its activities as processes. It requires the selection and organization of all activities as parts of a definite purposive scheme. At present the church scarcely can claim for its variety of activities a definite, unifying purpose. Societies, organizations, meetings, and exercises are adopted commonly, either under the impetus of tradition or for the sake of some immediate end. Many of them are justified only as means of maintaining the mechanism itself, keeping up the church organization or the church plant.

Allowing for the usual exceptions, is it unfair to say that the church commonly lacks a programme? It maintains traditional forms, it invents types of activity to meet transitory needs, or it develops a scheme of work designed principally to keep its organization alive, and to make it larger. The church must be as wise as this world. The manufacturer does not organize his plant principally for the sake of having a factory and increasing the number of wheels in motion. The church cannot afford to do that. It has too high a task. In the economy of things it is principally responsible for a product so precious it dare not waste time or dissipate energies. If its task is to develop spiritual persons it must discover how spiritual persons develop. They can grow only according to the laws of spiritual life. All the work of a church will be determined by these laws. These are the principles it must discover by patient study.

THE BASIS OF A PROGRAMME

Such a study does not lose sight of the divine elements; it does not ignore the working of the spirit of God. It simply seeks to discover and know the laws of life in order to do the work which lies in our hands. It asks what methods we must use to be in harmony with God ever working in his world. It takes the attitude of the wise farmer or horticulturist, who not only asks, What are the forces of nature—or of God—operating to grow things? but also, What are the things I must do to fit into that programme of nature? Our tendency, in the field where "God giveth the increase," is to spend ourselves in descriptions and definitions of the divine operations, instead of seeking to discover the principles upon which all our work must be based. Are we sure that what are called "means of grace" are really those means of grace—of growth into the grace, or character, of God—which are best? Have we discovered the right methods and all the methods, and are we making the most of them? If so, then all we can do is to work, to use them and have full faith as to the fruitage. Where men are loyal to God's laws of growth there can be no doubt as to results.

The parable from agriculture may be pressed further. The marvellous development of this field in the past two decades has been due to scientific inquiry into the laws of plant life. The great schools of agriculture have been and are steadily conducting studies to discover and apply the principles of life in their field. Science has served the farm and orchard with beneficent results. Science is simply reverent inquiry into truth, reverent endeavor to systematize knowledge and obey it. It has to be reverent, for it must approach all the facts without prejudice; it must always be ready to learn and implicitly to obey. Is it not possible, is it not our duty, to approach the field of the religious life in the same

reverent spirit? Is it conceivable that there are laws for
the lower life and none for the higher? Or is it possible we
must follow the one and can afford to ignore the other?

THE DUTY OF SCIENTIFIC KNOWLEDGE

The educational aim of the church has this third feature,
the recognition of a *religious method of development.* If man
was made to grow we may learn under what conditions and by
what methods this growth takes place. Otherwise there can
be no system, no real science nor plan of religious education.

If there is any truth in what here has been urged it evidently is the duty of every religious worker, of every minister, pastor, and teacher, to know the laws of religious development. These laws must dominate his work absolutely.
To ignore them is to waste his energies and to frustrate his
own purposes. Law reigns in the spiritual world. Wilful
ignorance is culpable neglect of duty. It is not only ignorance, it is irreverence. It is to attempt to do the work of
God by ways of our devising, to hope to do the work of the
spirit by man's cunning and skill. This is the capital irreverence of religion to-day, that we will not work in God's way.
We lack the patient, teachable reverence to discover truth;
we carelessly transgress the divine laws of the spiritual life.
We vainly expect results from methods of cheap devices,
patent schemes ignorantly concocted. We blindly follow
the tricks of spectacular mountebanks and charlatans, the
modern successful sorcerers. We fail to see the essential
irreverence of it all, the lazy indifference to truth, the snatch-
ing at quick results, the defiance of heavenly laws, the attempt to force the kingdom of heaven by the violence of
our machinery. Some urge: "But the devices succeed."

Do they? What is meant is not that they succeed in the ultimate purpose of religious work, but that they succeed in attracting attention, securing advertising, making money, and creating a sensation. Whatever measure of permanent success appears is usually due to an accidental following of divine law rather than to any honest effort to discover and obey it.

If a man would work in any field to-day he must know its laws. The engineer must know physics and mathematics. If he would deal with living things he must know the laws of life. The study of botany, biology, and plant chemistry may seem tedious to the aspiring agriculturist who is eager to produce crops, but in the end they fully demonstrate their value. Later he counts none of that time wasted, for he knows what to do, and when and why. He has certainty in his work. If he labors in another field, that of education, he finds the same patient study and investigation necessary. Indeed, the field of education is more difficult, for it is one of the latest of the sciences, it includes a larger number of factors, and the elements and operations do not so readily yield to investigation and classification. But scientific knowledge of the processes of human consciousness, of knowledge, reasoning, will, and action is growing steadily. So also this field of knowledge of man as a spiritual being is coming to have a more complete scientific basis. The laws of religious development are being more fully discovered. These laws are the working principles for all those who are religious teachers and leaders. They are the laws upon which the work of a church must be based.

The function of religious education in a church implies, then, the adoption of a clearly defined programme for the development of religious persons in a religious society, based upon faith in life as growth, conducted upon the discoverable laws under which religious persons grow and a religious society is organized, and guided by leaders trained in and obedient to these laws.

ADVANTAGES IN THE CHURCH

The church has peculiar advantages as an educational institution; in its very nature as an organization it possesses some of the ideal conditions for education. First, it has an advantage as a society. Education is a social process. Modern education seeks to provide in the school natural social relations and conditions. In the life of a church these conditions are already established. Persons are brought together under a variety of relationships; they learn to live together. Second, the church has the advantage of indirection; the educational process goes forward largely unconsciously. The institution is not labelled as a school. Third, it has the advantage of ideal aims. Through all its social life the members feel the attraction of high purposes and noble concepts. Fourth, its work furnishes ample opportunity for activities which are commonly simple outgrowths of the social relationships and the high ideals. The work furnishes expressional activities which are free from consciousness of the educational purpose. Fifth, the greater part of instruction may be most closely related to experience. It becomes an essential part of life. Sixth, it reaches all kinds of persons all through their lives. Its curriculum need know no bounds of age or of condition.

The church fully realizes its opportunity and discharges its function in the degree that it organizes all its activities for the development of the lives of persons as social, religious beings. Under this ideal we turn to study the varied organizations and activities of a church as educational opportunities.

REFERENCES

EDUCATION THROUGH THE CHURCH

COE, GEORGE ALBERT, *A Social Theory of Religious Education* (Scribners, 1917). An indispensable study.

—— *Education in Religion and Morals* (Revell, 1904).

BUSHNELL, HORACE, *Christian Nurture* (Scribners, revised edition, 1917). The classic presenting the fundamental argument for religious education.

WILM, EMIL CARL, *The Culture of Religion* (Pilgrim Press, 1912).

RELIGIOUS EDUCATION ASSOCIATION, *The Improvement of Religious Education* (Convention papers, 1903).

—— *The Aims of Religious Education* (Convention papers, 1905).

FAUNCE, W. H. P., *The Educational Ideal and the Ministry* (Macmillan, 1908).

GAILOR, T. F., *The Christian Church and Education* (Whittaker, 1910).

FAUNCE, W. H. P., and WILLETT, HERBERT L., "Church and Religious Education," *Religious Education,* vol. IV, pp. 527–541.

SOUTHWORTH, F. C., article in *Religious Education* for December, 1916, p. 477.

SCIENTIFIC BASIS OF RELIGIOUS EDUCATION

COE, G. A., *The Psychology of Religion* (Univ. of Chicago Press, 1916). One of the most important recent works; essential to any thorough study.

AMES, EDWARD S., *The Psychology of Religious Experience* (Houghton Mifflin, 1910). A comprehensive study.

WATERHOUSE, E. S., *The Psychology of the Christian Life* (Chas. H. Kelly, 1913). A fairly simple introduction.

JAMES, WILLIAM, *The Varieties of Religious Experience* (Longmans, Green, 1902). A classic on the subject. It analyzes the different types of experience as revealed in a large number of cases drawn from literature, history, and current observation.

STARBUCK, EDWIN D., *The Psychology of Religion* (Scribners, 1899). The first book to study the phenomena of conversion.

CHAPTER V

THE FUNCTION OF PUBLIC WORSHIP

PUBLIC worship is the one outstanding, common activity of all churches. However much they may differ in creed and in ritual, the day of rest is the day of greatest activity for them all, and services of worship, of widely varying forms, are the principal occupation of the day. We take for granted the Sunday-morning church-bells and the companies of well-dressed persons on their way to services. A stranger would assume that this was one of our national or racial institutions. Until very recently it has been so embedded in social habit as to require no further sanction than that of tradition.

Do the churches conduct Sunday services of worship largely as a matter of social habit? If not, what is the history of this custom? Few are so thoughtful, or presumptuous, as to inquire whether there is any rational basis, any adequate purpose, in the custom. One is expected to "attend" church—mark the significance of the current phrase "attend church"—just as one is expected to wear certain kinds of clothes at certain times. In many places, especially in rural districts, there is serious doubt as to the respectability of persons who do not attend worship in some church at least once every Sunday. A variety of reasons may be given for this expectation, but custom is its strongest argument. It is regarded as a good habit, one associated with "Sunday clothes" and with the distinctions of the day of rest. When the inquiring mind asks, Why? the answers seem to falter. Apostolic injunctions will be quoted, but with little evidence of pertinency. Ecclesiastical authority will be cited and tradition may be urged, but these do not give the reason why. Yet the evident bearing of all argument is that the service of worship is the principal function of the church and that one can hardly be a true member of the church and neglect these services.

The attitude of the public toward public worship, however, shows that a rather clear and definite concept of its purpose and meaning exists to-day. The public expects that these services shall be attractive, that they shall constitute a mild form of diversion respectably labelled as religion, and many churches definitely cater to this expectation. If the services are advertised the appeal is made to the reader by striking topics of sermons, or it is based upon the high quality of entertainment. Seldom does one read any reference to worship. In every way the passer-by is assured that he will be entertained. In fact, we have become accustomed to seeing churches compete for popular attendance with commercialized amusements and use some of the same inducements. The man on the street judges the service of worship by the quality of the musical programme or by the ability of the speaker to make him forget the passage of time. He is not alone to blame for such criteria, for the church has been busy promising him that she could and would meet them. At least, in many communions she has created the current idea of the church service as a form of entertainment suitable to the day of religion.

WHAT HAS BECOME OF WORSHIP?

Stranger still, at least in the light of history, is the attitude of church-members toward the Sunday services of worship. Their concepts can fairly be inferred by the elements which they select for commendation and by their characteristic current comments. Evidently, to many the service is simply a programme of music, diversified by prayer and reading, and ending with oratory. For large numbers the music is the important and most attractive feature, and the work of the choir or soloists is the centre of their interests. To others, especially to the older generation, the attraction lies in the eloquence of the minister. These, music and oratory, are the two things on which popular pride is based; these are the two magnets by which the church expects to draw in the outsiders. In many non-liturgical churches the minister is selected, or "called," almost solely on the basis of his powers of oratory. If it comes to pass that these powers decline, if he ceases to be an "attractive preacher," the church will grow restive and discontented and he will receive hints that other fields need him more than this one. Is it not also true that in the ordering of such churches one of the most serious, perplexing, and often divisive questions is that of the music and its leaders, creators, or performers, as the case may be? There are three church committees that turn the hair gray—they are "Pulpit," "Music," and "Finance."

Is the decline in church attendance to be attributed wholly to a growing spirit of irreligion? Is it not rather that men turn from that which is neither worship nor amusement, though it attempts or pretends to be both? If we advertise bread and offer only stones, is it likely that we can long hold the multitude? Of many a church service it may well be said: "God is not in all their thoughts." Before we denounce the godlessness of the times we might well inquire as to the real godliness of our own organized religious life.

One must always be cautious with generalities—there are many churches where worship is real and deeply reverent. But is it unfair to say that, no matter what the variety of other activities may be and no matter what the quality of reverence may be, in a great number of non-liturgical churches to-day the Sunday services constitute the centre about which all the life revolves, the principal affair of the church, and that in these services the two outstanding, dominating features are a musical programme and a sermon? Is it unfair to say that in the minds of by far the greater number of persons the first, great commandment is that these two features, music and oratory, shall be attractive or entertaining?

In the liturgical churches the situation is somewhat different, though here it is quite evident that often there is keen consciousness of the advertising quality and drawing power of musical programmes. But the real danger lies in another direction. The liturgy is rich in stimulus for worship; but all its power may be lost if it is followed in a blind, mechanical manner. Wherever the conduct of worship is thoughtless it must be irreverent. There is also the danger that the dignity of the ritual and the riches of symbolism shall be emphasized for their immediate spectacular effect rather than for their tremendous powers of spiritual development through worship.

WHY SUNDAY SERVICES?

The question remains, Why conduct or hold these Sunday services? What purpose do they serve? If we mean anything by calling them services of worship, what is the purpose of worship? What is the underlying idea of worship? Even when we get away from the thought of presenting an attractive programme, what idea of worship remains? The problem of public worship must be faced squarely. The first question ought to be, Why? To what end is it instituted and maintained? It must justify its demands on time. It must establish its right to a place in the programme of the church.

Frequently the answer would be that religious people ought to worship God because he is God, because it is a duty we owe him. We talk of pleasing him with our praises, of bringing offerings of song and adoration to him. We tend to think of a God who demands our prostration in recognition of his greatness and power. When services of worship are thus regarded in their fundamental aspects they become as the offerings of bulls and rams on ancient altars. Is it the case that we assemble in churches to satisfy the pride of the Jehovah god? Is this what services of worship mean?

Undoubtedly, much superstition remains even in Christian churches, but there are few who would openly avow the motive of sacrificial tribute. We are conscious of the inadequacy of this answer. A ceremonial of obeisance before the Almighty can be but a craven, perfunctory affair. A public act of prostration will be only formal and exterior. It is essentially contrary to our idea of a God who calls us to draw near, not by crawling in the dust, but as children who look into a Father's face. Public worship is surely more than a ministry to the pride of the Deity.

WHAT IS WORSHIP?

Worship rises out of our need; it obeys an inner imperative rather than any external authority. It is the outreach of our lives. It is our search for natural relations with wider, higher spiritual life. Because we hunger for life we seek means of communion with God as the life of all. In real life every soul hungers for righteousness. We need encouragement. We need ideals to lift up our hearts and strengthen our hands. And we need to feel the strength of the many who have common needs and common hopes. Worship is a need of the social spirit seeking communion with other spirits on its highest levels. Worship is a need of personal life seeking fellowship with the Person who is Life. Worship is man's search for the society of God. We meet to worship God, not because he needs our praises, but because we need the stimulus, the inspiring, the up-pull of the consciousness of the divine reality, of the things that are before us.

But even when the thought of worship is lifted to the level of sincere adoration and communion the public services often seem to have little relation to this great experience. Surely, if we think of God as the Father with whom we would always dwell, it must sound strange to issue a weekly call for an hour of communion with him. And, even if that be the purpose, how little does the programme provided stimulate any such communion! Indeed, is not the sense of unreality in communion due to the artificial and perverted nature of most services of worship? Would it not be possible to have such public assemblies as would meet deep needs of our natures and experiences in such a way that we would not have to be coaxed to them, but would with difficulty be kept from them?

WHY PUBLIC WORSHIP?

Public worship is social utilization of the accumulated spiritual life, the use of the emotions and aspirations of the many for the life of each. Social impulses, stimuli, and realizations are stronger than individual ones. Two or three met in His name are stronger, see more clearly and keenly, feel more deeply, resolve more highly than two or three thinking separately in His name. There is the method and motive. We meet because each one is more when with others than when alone. Social forces are at work. A group is, as a group, seeking larger and richer life. Here, in such processes, is the clew to the ordering of a service of worship. It must be thought out in terms of effect, stimulus, and growth in the lives of worshippers. In other words, worship is an educational process—because it has to do with a social group seeking growth—and its conduct is an educational problem.

THE EDUCATIONAL PROCESS

An educational concept of the service of worship does not imply its conversion into an academic occasion, nor does it mean that it exists only or primarily for purposes of instruction. It does mean that we think of it as directed to the development of the lives of persons.

In public worship the church is engaged in religious education through certain definite and easily understood processes. These are: *First,* the association of persons for a common purpose; *second,* the direction of the minds of these persons toward certain stimulating ideas and ideals; and, *third,* the controlled development of the emotions of this group in the directions desirable for their growth as religious persons. The whole purpose is that men and women together may be lifted in thought and feeling in order that they may desire and love, that they may will and realize finer, richer, more Godlike lives and service in a wider, richer world.

GROWTH BY ASSOCIATION

The first step in religious education by worship is the association of persons for a common purpose. "The assembling of yourselves" has an educational sanction. Two people associated are never the same as they were when separate or as they would have been remaining separate. The parts of a crowd are never the same in the crowd as they are alone.* The very fact of gathering in a social group moves the feeling, enriches and widens the sympathies and the view of life. The public assembly for worship lifts men out of the individual and solitary into the social and universal. The group becomes conscious of a common purpose, and the fact of the common purpose enhances its meaning and value. This is the answer to the man who says he worships best when alone. The consciousness of spiritual reality is possible to the individual when alone. But if the experience is real it becomes at once a social experience; he as a

* For a simple statement of crowd psychology, see George A. Coe in *Psychology of Religion,* p. 120. For further study, see Le Bon, *The Crowd,* chap. IV.

person, a spiritual being, is with his God, his Father, the Father of spirits. But in the church service where worship is a reality he is with the larger family. His own realization is quickened by the fact that this spiritual communion is a reality to so many others. Worship is, then, in the church, first, an act of the social consciousness of spiritual reality. It would appear that the ideal church service would emphasize this social communion on the spiritual plane and that every church service of worship might be tested by its mediation of divine fellowship and communion to us.*

We do well to keep in mind the special power of public worship through the force of *social idealization*. The educational purpose begins in gathering the group for the expression of its common social relationships. It is carried forward as the group realizes its unity as one family having one spiritual, social life by which it is one with God, a life that makes all living divine, all relationships sacred, and all work worship. The effect of such social worship is both to create the new society of God's family and to train men for its life everywhere. The question that is sure to arise—Shall we then abandon the sermon from this service?—will be considered in the section on teaching. Just now we are emphasizing the primary purpose of public worship which is realized by the very act of organizing a social group for that purpose.

The physical conditions will be such as to interpret or suggest the special social significance of the gathering. Evidently, the room must be more than an auditorium, a

---

* It may be worth while to note that these chapters were written before Professor Coe's inspiring treatment of the theme appeared in *A Social Theory of Religious Education*.

place designed primarily in order that with ease and comfort we may hear some one person speak; it must literally be a meeting-place. The form, arrangement, seating, lighting, and adornment ought to express clearly the dominant purpose, that many might become one in the feeling, thought, and attitude of fellowship and communion.* Here for a while they gather in the reality and explicit form of relationships that are held as ideal and implicit in all life, the relationships of the one family of God. This is not a listening group, pulpit-centric; it is more like a family group. Its unity is not through lines of interest converging on a common centre, the preacher, but through ties of a common relationship in the spiritual life. Is anything more needed to-day than that we shall feel deeply and be controlled in all life by the reality of our unity, love, and obligations as the common family of God? Where there is a vital social reality in worship it will carry over into all social life. If on these special occasions men meet in conscious spiritual unity, those relationships become dominant in daily life. They are both stimulated and habituated toward the maintenance of those relations in every-day life. In the deepening realization of spiritual fellowship men do truly worship God, for, as they love their brethren they become like him, they glorify him by knowing and loving one another.

ORGANIZING THE SOCIAL MIND

The second step of religious education through public worship is the unifying and directing of the minds of the

---

* The Religious Education Association will send, on application, a pamphlet of information on plans educationally conceived, giving names of architects and references to books.

persons in the group toward stimulating ideas and ideals. We might call this *the organization of the many and varied stimuli of worship*. These stimuli operate here precisely as they do under other conditions in life. Ideas come to us through the nerves, through eyes and ears, by touch and odor, through colors and forms, through words in print, spoken or sung. The ideas thus received stir the feelings, quicken the imagination, find relations to other ideas, and stimulate us to action. They excite feelings, pleasurable or otherwise, and they move us either toward or from the actions suggested.

Essentially, this is teaching, for this process is the very centre of the teacher's task. The aim in teaching is to so stimulate the mind as to secure a reaction in feeling, judgment, conviction, and action. The main consideration is that the stimulus, whatever it may be, shall lead to the appropriate and desired action. The movement toward action is all that the persons stimulated need to recognize. No teaching is teaching that does not carry over to the pupil's life of action.

The direction of worship is a most serious responsibility: it involves the power to play on the very springs of life, to control emotions, and to color the judgment of many. It calls for a high sense of responsibility. Its possibilities should make any man pause. In ignorance, with excellent intentions, he may do irreparable damage to lives. One must know what he is doing. He must know how the emotions are stimulated, how the will is directed and strengthened. He must know to what ends he would direct every dynamic of action.

He who leads in worship is doing much more than direct-

ing a performance. He is playing upon many minds: he
is stirring imaginations, stimulating feelings; he is turning
the hearts of his people toward God until they all have one
heart and one mind. In order that he may do this he must
examine with care every part of the service. He must determine the purpose and the power of every act of the worshippers, and every influence that comes upon them. No
part may be perfunctorily adopted or thoughtlessly done.

THE POWER OF THE CONCRETE

To be explicit: every leader of worship ought to stop to
examine the values, for worship purposes, of a picture, a
stained-glass window, or an altar-cloth. He ought to study
the general effect of interior arrangements and decorations.
All that appeals to the eye constitutes forms of very active
stimulation. We tend to forget this and imagine that education is effected only through the ear. This is far from
being the case with children. They hear relatively little;
they see much and, although habits of minute and detailed
observation may not have been established, the salient impressions of objects are very vivid. With the adult, conditions of worship depend less on concrete environment, the
things felt and seen, than with children. But the effect of
visible objects is very direct and often lasting. This should
suggest the wisdom of object-and-sense-teaching through
architecture, picture, color, and form especially designed,
not to meet the captious criteria of adult art forms, but to
satisfy youth's need of religious stimulation and direction.
And here the guiding question would be, To what forms of
action does the feeling of this picture or form ultimately
lead? It is evident that no precise formulæ can be given.

We do not know that if one sees one kind of picture he will at once go out and do one specific act, or that another art form will lead to some other act. But we do know that certain colors, forms, harmonies, and other visual appeals tend to make one feel that life is beautiful and that we must keep it so, that certain ways of living—harmoniously, calmly, patiently—are desirable, and that therefore we must seek those ways.

How steadily, forcibly, loudly do things preach to the young while words fall unheeded! Is it not worth while to catch some sense of the value of the sermon that is not spoken but is felt and seen? It is no small element in worship for all. It lies in order, harmony, serenity of action, cleanliness, beauty of form and color. It lies as much in the manner in which things are done as in the fixed colors and shapes about them. It lies within the chapel and meeting-house as well as in the cathedral. The character of religion to many is mediated through the concrete, through that which most immediately strikes the senses. And for every one these appeals to eye and other senses co-operate to form the complete impression. We cannot afford to allow anything that would lessen or detract to have a place here. Every form of impression must be made to co-operate and to serve the ultimate purpose of the service of worship.*

MUSIC

So much attention has been given to the concrete principally because it is the aspect of worship most commonly

* There are valuable suggestions in the papers by Ralph A. Cram, James S. Pray, and Waldo S. Pratt, in *The Aims of Religious Education* (The Religious Education Association, 1905). The one consideration,

slighted. This emphasis will serve to indicate the care with which each part of worship must be studied. It seems almost unnecessary to plead for loyalty to educational principles in the choice of the hymns. But in many services it is evident that if the hymns have been chosen at all, no principle has been followed in their selection. Singing together should be thinking, feeling, and aspiring together. Often it should be both social aspiration and determination. How important, then, that the leader shall select the sentiments he desires to see developed! We can all remember with ease more hymns than sermons. This is due not alone to repetition but also to the poetic form of the hymn, the musical setting, and the fact of singing as a social exercise.

The literary form of the hymn may have as great an influence as its thought. Aspiration demands the best. The sentiment that ennobles must have associations of elevating language. Doggerel and slang may have apparent advantages in their every-day familiarity for some people, but such associations of thought and custom hinder more than they help. If the life is to move forward it needs the associations of higher levels. The exercise of worship must lead the spirit to reach up.

So with every part of the worship. All are parts of a common purpose. Whatever it be—reading, responses, hymns, chants, prayers, or offering—these persons who participate are not the same as they were before. Something has happened in them. Worship is possible only when the

whether in designing a new building or improving an old one, should be that every part shall express a religious purpose and all parts shall unite in this expression.

parts of a service are directed and unified to secure certain results in persons and when those results turn men toward God, toward doing his will, and lead them in the direction of his law. It is worship whenever we yield ourselves to persuasions, feelings, and aspirations that both make us long after godliness and cause us to stretch forth ourselves in doing the will of the Most High.

GUIDANCE TOWARD A GOAL

If the leader of worship is loyal to the educational ideal he will seek to control the minds and emotions of the group *toward certain definite ends*. Every part of the service will be chosen as a part of a real purpose. The leader leads somewhere. He must have an aim clearly defined. The emotional stimulus of worship must be purposeful and not an end in itself. There is a common tendency to think of worship simply as a state of feeling, without regard to any further end. Emotion as an end in itself soon fails; its powers of response are deadened; it dies for lack of expression in action. The emotions can never be used wisely unless they are directed toward right ends. If an emotional state is regarded as the desired end, the stimulus will be chosen with reference to that end alone. The process will end in itself and no progress will be made.

To take a simple instance, in selecting a hymn or in directing its singing in worship what should be considered—the kinds of feelings likely to be quickened or created by the hymn or the kinds of things those who sing are likely to do, or to do more or do better through this singing? Many hymns are selected for worship without either question being asked and there is no special intent or consideration of values in the selection. But, if there is definite intent, the answer would be that both questions must be asked, but that the first inevitably leads to the second—What sort of actions will follow the feelings stimulated by this hymn? Therefore each hymn will be chosen with the goal of life in mind.

In worship the minister is leading his people toward the life of a divine society. He has in mind not only what they will think and how they feel but what they will do about it all. He is educating them in the degree that he is leading out their lives. The test of worship is in work in the everyday world. Worship makes the world. Moving men toward God is moving all life toward the divine ideal.

This is what the minister of the church is seeking to do in the service of worship. He is the "master of assemblies," not as one who merely manages a number of separate parts but who organizes the unified social life before him. He leads the assembly as a unit. He stimulates them all in order that all, as a whole, may produce more life in each and in all. He is developing lives. The function of worship is realized in the educational process of the development of lives by the interplay and reaction of vital powers. Worship becomes a means; the end sought is worth, that is, more worthy men and women, because they have meditated upon, they have communed with, they have felt and seen, the invisible.

REFERENCES

HARTSHORNE, HUGH, *Worship in the Sunday School* (Teachers College, 1913).

HOYT, A. S., *Public Worship for Non-Liturgical Churches* (Doran, 1911).

HYLAN, JOHN P., *Public Worship* (Open Court, 1901). A psychological study on a questionnaire basis.

CHAPTER VI

CONGREGATIONAL TEACHING *

TEACHING is the act of stimulating the feelings, guiding the perception, convincing the judgment, and moving the will so as to produce a desired action. In our practical use of the word we tend to confine this process to the worker or the teacher who stands before a class. That always has been one of the most efficient forms of teaching in the church. The earliest congregations seem to have used that method for the instruction of the young.† The modern church provides, on Sundays and on other occasions, for teaching small groups. One cannot overemphasize the importance of this work. But a detailed study of class teaching in the church belongs to those works which treat of church-school methods. We seek here to call attention to the opportunities of teaching in the church service of worship. Not all the teaching work of the church is done in its classes. We have seen already that it is going on in associated worship; we shall see that it is being effected through play and organized activity, and we know that the voice of the true preacher is the voice of a teacher.

* In this chapter attention is confined to the ministry of teaching in relation to worship. In Chapter XV the needs of young people are considered, and in Chapters XIX and XX some attention is paid to the ministry of teaching through classes and like organizations.

† On the history of teaching in the church, see the author's *Evolution of the Sunday School*, 1911.

TEACHING BY PREACHING

At its best, preaching is prophesying. The minister in the pulpit stands in the order of all those who have stood in the splendid light of glowing vision and called men to the light. The prophets are they who reach our consciences, who quicken our purposes, who make us lift our dull eyes to see truth and God. Prophesying is teaching at its best. It is not prediction—it is declaration—it is the declaration of the divine directed to the consciences and conduct of men. It seeks, not to satisfy puerile curiosity regarding the future, but to determine the future by stimulating and guiding the lives of men. The prophet is one who sees what ought to be, who feels that divine imperative, and who seeks to make it real by declaring it.

The minister of the church is its educational leader, for his chief function is that of prophetic leadership. He directs the organization of the whole in order that it may co-operate with the purpose he declares in his teaching, the doing of the will of God in the ways of men. He is the chief teacher, for he must interpret this whole purpose to all, he must quicken their feelings so that it becomes desirable; he must persuade their minds so that it is clear; he must direct their wills so that this programme becomes theirs in choice and practice.

Preaching is teaching. Its aims are vastly higher than those of entertainment. The full significance of the teaching function must be restored to the work of preaching. Preaching must be redeemed from its debasing competition with the arts of amusement or entertainment. The pulpit cannot afford any longer to cater to those thrifty souls who do not think of buying a seat at an entertainment house so long as they can get what they like for nothing at the church. By lasting insistence on greater aims and responsibilities we must free ourselves from the custom of engaging the leader of the whole life of the church on the basis of his ability to draw the crowd and to entertain the otherwise indifferent masses.

Preaching is teaching. It is vastly greater and finer than the dissemination of knowledge. The preacher must know and the people must learn; but the ability to put information into alluring language does not of itself make the teacher. Of course the knowledge must be there—nothing can be accomplished without it. It is the essential means; but it is only the means. Preaching that is merely informational will not be transformational, but preaching never will transform unless it informs. The teacher uses knowledge as a means. It is his tool and not his product. He is not proud of his learning, though he justly may be proud of its effects in the lives of those whom he teaches.

LEARNING TO TEACH

Preaching is teaching because it is founded on fundamental educational processes. It is proclamation, declaration, and information for the purposes of stimulation, transformation, and action. Any one who would preach must know something of these processes—he must know what takes place in the minds and wills of those who hear. It scarcely seems necessary to-day to insist that the preacher ought to know not only how sermons are prepared but also what happens as the sermon goes out to the hearers. How else can he intelligently prepare? He plays upon the human instrument;

he will be a guilty bungler, committing it may be fatal errors, if he be ignorant of the laws of that instrument. Those who decry or deride the study of psychology for the minister simply assert that the workman does better when he knows nothing of either his tools or his materials. It takes time and it costs labor to know this material of personality —to understand its processes and to become master of its ways. It is much easier to make sermons than it is to know souls. But your sermon is wasted if you do not know how to find the way to the souls of men. Does some one say that Savonarola, Finney, Beecher, and Moody knew nothing of psychology? Then some one is wrong. They certainly knew much; they learned in the schools that were open to them. They studied men. They were keen observers of lives. We can be sure were they living they would take advantage of every source of knowledge now open to them, and they would accept the help of every patient investigator into the laws of this life of consciousness.

He who would be a teacher must be willing to pay the teacher's price. A teacher is not alone one who learns a lesson; he must be one who learns lives. Life is the material in which he works. All learning and literature he uses, but by means of them he makes life.

THE CALL FOR THE TEACHER

True preaching is teaching that commands the place of the prophet. He is a preacher who wakes men and stirs them to discover their spiritual rights and their spiritual opportunities. The preaching that drives a man out to do something for the vision he has seen leaves him no time to analyze æsthetic reactions, to determine whether he was pleased or whether the sermon was a credit to that church. It cures a church of the entertainment delusion. Preaching that is educationally efficient produces effects. It causes men to do. And that is what men hunger for to-day. They seek the stimulus of life. They see glimpses of a glorious vision through the rifts in clouds of oratory. Their hearts hunger for its realization; their hands are lifted to its work, and, alas, there the matter ends, for there the sermon ends. The preaching stopped short of teaching because it had no terminus in life or in realization. The preacher who has seen a vision should also know how to make men both see and realize it.

This, then, is the preacher's teaching function: that men, as spiritual beings, may know and do the truth, that they may discover and realize the full riches of the spiritual life, and that they may seek to have all the world experience that life. He is to lead lives into the experience of the family of God. This is the peculiar function of the preacher; he is the one recognized teacher and specialist in religion. To him men are still looking for the word regarding God. What shall we think of him, and where shall we find him? Is he the Jahveh of olden days, the mighty thunderer who seems blindly to blast the forest-oaks and devastate our little crops? Is he some far-off potentate, the one king remaining when all other kings pass into history? The men who speak about God wait for the teacher in the church to answer their questions. The men who do not speak of God, who shrink from the popular interpretations of the word, who say there is no God as they would say "there are no gods," still look for one who will reveal God. They seek an answer to questions which are fundamentally the same as those of the other group: What is the meaning of life? Who will show us its plan and help us find its lasting values?

The preacher is the teacher of righteousness. Life is all school to living men and each day's experience brings its new problems. In the pressure of the business world it is easy to forget some of the essential factors. We are likely to seek solutions only in the light of economics and politics and forget that man is more than the things he has. The teacher must so insistently bring to us the reality of the spiritual in every fact of life that we shall never forget it. The minister so teaches life that we habitually think of it not merely as a wage-earning, house-dwelling affair, but as something primarily possessing eternal worths. This teacher has to save us from absorption in barn-building and keep us from losing ourselves in our things. He has to interpret this daily life of affairs in the light of all affairs and all days. He must set the eternal in our hearts.

Do these needs not call for a teacher? And how shall one teach in the face of such needs who is unwilling to learn the laws of teaching? The orator may be born, but the teacher must be trained. The greater the responsibility of the teacher the greater the need for training. The professional schools for the ministry are recognizing this need. They are specializing in scientific knowledge in this field and they are offering courses in the different technical aspects of religious education.* For those who are already engaged in their professional work, reading and correspondence

* For a survey of the work available in theological seminaries, see the article by Frank G. Ward in *Religious Education* for October, 1915, at p. 426.

courses are available.* Something much more rigorous than desultory reading will be necessary. They who would teach must pay the high price of patient, painstaking learning.

RELATION TO WORSHIP

There is no fixed line between the function of worship and that of teaching. *True worship teaches, true teaching stimulates worship.* The sermon that teaches is a proper and essential part of the service of worship. This unity is quite fundamental. The sermon is more than an intellectual exercise and the service is more than an emotional experience. Both should have both elements; both are essentially educational experiences, leading to action and life. It is a serious mistake to speak, as we sometimes do, of worship as "opening exercises," evidently regarding them as a vestibule to the intellectual mansion, the sermon.

But some one says the sermon is the means for the impartation of ideas. That is precisely the trouble with many sermons; at least there are two kinds of sermons that miss fire—those that are not troubled with ideas and those that are nothing but ideas. We have been insisting that the sermon teaches only as it does much more than impart knowledge. It is efficient as it is essentially a part of the whole service of worship. It must be directed to the same end as the prayer and reading and singing. It is to be judged by its power in stimulating persons to know and feel and act. In all the public services, including the sermon, the leader must be considering what is taking place

* The American Institute of Sacred Literature offers an especially good course for ministers. The Religious Education Association, Chicago, will send, free, lists of books.

in the minds of the people. And not only what changes take place in the ideas of the hearers, but what changes take place in them, in their whole selves. How are they different? What changes have occurred in their feelings, their ideas, their judgments, their will, and their actions?

We tend to think of the earlier Christian congregations as gatherings about the personality of an apostle with a burning message. That was true only of the first public assemblages. The regular gatherings of believers, in houses, barns, or catacombs, were bound together by the ties of a new social life. They meant something wonderful, new, and refreshing when they said "Brother" and "Sister." They met under the power of the new ideals of a common family, a new society. Our emphasis on preaching, which has led to the currency of the phrase "church auditorium," has overshadowed the greater, dominant purpose of social worship. It has succeeded in obscuring the idea of the Christian family in its assembly. It accounts for the very common phrase descriptive of all public services as "preaching services." The result is that many come, not to worship in the joy of an ideal social life that looks in love to a Father's face, but to listen to an address. Naturally, they demand that the address shall be entertaining; if it is not they will turn to another and more attractive orator elsewhere.

The professional training of the minister of religion is partly responsible for the overshadowing of worship by oratory. In many schools he is still taught that the first great duty before him is to be a preacher. The young seminary student, under this instruction and under the traditions of the school, cherishes the hope of being the "star preacher" of his class. Pulpit eloquence is what the people want, and the preacher is trained to meet the demand. But, unfortunately, the demand dictates the nature of the supply. The people crave the pleasing sensations of oratory. The eloquence that entertains and thrills becomes an end in itself. The teaching purpose is forgotten in the oratorical process. Worship degenerates from the educational direction of a social group toward developing ideals and experiences into the elaboration of a verbal masterpiece framed in the accessories of prayer and hymns.

THE MINISTRY OF PREACHING

But there is a reason for the dominance of the sermon which goes back of the current customs of professional training for the ministry. It lies in the fact that there is a ministry of preaching, that the spoken word is still to some degree the most effective method of disseminating knowledge, of declaring the good news, and that the will, judgments, and feelings are reached by this means. We cannot forget the place of preaching in the early spread of Christianity, nor its place in the growth of modern churches and in our own religious experience.

Two considerations are to be borne in mind. *First:* That preaching and worship may be one and the same, but that the special method of the former must not be permitted to change the nature of the latter. Preaching is only a part of worship. *Second:* That to-day the method of preaching does not hold quite the same place as in the past. The spoken word is not the only method of disseminating truth. The time was when, for nearly all the people, all knowledge came by the spoken word—readers were few and books were fewer. The man who passed the week with little or no intellectual or emotional food came with keen appetite for the Sunday's long sermons. To-day all those who read, who do more than expose themselves to the newspaper head-lines, are being preached to daily by the hour through books, pamphlets, magazines, even by moving pictures and the drama. Not all this preaching is spiritual, though more of it may have this quality than we suspect; but in any case it is all preaching, proclaiming, stimulating the mind and feel-ings. It is thus tending to make the sermon not only an additional burden, an offering to a surfeited mind, but also to make the sermon less necessary. Our sole dependence is no longer on this mode of reaching the mind.

Shall we then abandon the sermon and leave the teach-ing function to classes and to the printed page? By no means. We still need that prophetic teaching which is possible only with the large assemblage. Preaching is teaching a class which has been lifted, prepared, and stimu-lated by its social worship. It is instruction lifted to its higher power by the social life of the assemblage. The one way to meet the competition of the printed page is to give to this preaching the qualities which cold type cannot have. The sermon is teaching at its best, because it presents a per-son to persons. The man and the message are one in teach-ing men.

The special function of preaching is that of unifying and directing worship: controlling and directing the emotions of the group for the ultimate ends of worship. Preaching presents a focal point for all the emotions. As the service and the environment stimulate persons—"move" them, to use a current word—preaching presents the ends toward which they may move. Here are multitudes, perhaps deeply stirred, moving as sheep not having a shepherd, filled with desire and longing, but all inchoate, without direction. The sermon carries forward the work of worship; by the control of thought it gathers up all the flood of emotions and directs them toward worthy ends. It takes lives that are stimulated and leads them toward the realization of their ideals and so toward God. This is worship, in that it is the organization of the life of all toward the ideal and its realization. This is teaching, in the degree that it stimulates lives, that it leads to the deeds of the religious life.

The service of worship is designed to secure an impressive, effective realization of the divine love and the divine glory of life. It moves and guides us toward that glory as our highest good. It reveals the greatest good of all in a world of God's will. It compels us to seek this good, to realize it in all life, in the conditions and order of all life. The minister, having organized the service in order that all together, with the cumulative effect of the congregation, might feel the power and desirability of godliness, now, by means of the sermon, directs their feelings and shows how the ideal may be realized. He focusses and guides the sum of social and spiritual feeling. He seeks to guide the emotional content of worship—the sense of a social life, of difference, of joy and elevation—so that it may have definiteness of impression and may pass over into reality through action. Preaching precipitates emotion in conduct and so realizes the whole purpose of worship in that the worshipper becomes more like him whom he worships. Men are changed, not by what they feel, but by the feeling passing over into doing, so that the beauty of the feeling becomes a part of themselves. So preaching is teaching, causing men to see and do. It is prophesying as it reveals God's will and causes it to be realized.

REFERENCES

FAUNCE, W. H. P., *The Educational Ideal in the Ministry* (Macmillan, 1908).

MARK, THISTLETON, *The Pedagogics of Preaching* (Revell, 1911).

PEPPER, G. W., *A Voice from the Crowd* (Yale Press, 1915).

CHAPTER VII

THE FUNCTION OF EVANGELISM

THE church is essentially an evangelizing agency. Its work is to save the world. The full admission of that fact and insistence upon it in no way invalidates the fundamental thesis of this book. The educational aim concentrates the energies of the church in leading men to the realization of the divine likeness in themselves and the divine will in a social order. Fully to do this is to save the world, and to do anything else is not evangelism. Any work which does not seek to bring men to the personal fulness and to the social perfection which Jesus taught and exhibited falls short of the work of evangelism.

The assumption that there is a sharp conflict between the educational aim and the evangelistic aim is based on a misunderstanding of one of the two, usually on ignorance of both. But so common is this assumption that it becomes necessary to face it and to look clearly at the aims of education and of evangelism. Examination will convince us that when fully understood they are both exactly the same.

THE TWO AIMS

The evangelistic aim seeks the salvation of all men. Its message is the good news that God desires man's salvation from sin and his full entrance into the divine family. Its method principally is the declaration of this good news. The aim is accomplished when each man everywhere knows

78

himself as the child of God and seeks to live fully in the family relations implied. *The educational aim* seeks the development of all men into fulness of religious character; that is, in simple terms, the salvation of all men. Its method uses whatever, in accordance with the laws under which lives grow, will effect this purpose. The aims in both cases are the same, except that education is more likely to go farther and pass from individual salvation to social rightness.

If the aims are the same and the methods so in consonance, how does conflict appear? When persons of different mental habits discuss the same thing divergencies are often more evident than agreements. "Evangelism" is the slogan of one group habituated to emphasize one aspect; "education" is the slogan of another group, accustomed to think in different terms. The former emphasizes results; the latter methods. The former is likely to cleave to accepted forms and definitions; the latter to seek out modern terms. Persons of evangelistic fervor and habit of mind are ready to assume that the educational method must be wrong because it uses what is to them unfamiliar language. But it is simply trying to find terms that express with exactness, in the language of to-day, just what really happens in the minds and wills of men. It is unwilling to use phrases, cherished for their past service, and now often handled without clear consciousness of meaning. It dares to do what Jesus did— forsake traditional forms of words and say things that mean something to men of the current hour.

OBJECTIONS TO THE EDUCATIONAL IDEAL

But the essential difficulty for many in thinking of the educational method in religion lies in their assumption that it deals only with knowledge. "How can any one hope," they inquire, "that souls will be saved by knowledge? Has not the pride of intellect in itself always been a snare to the soul and a source of sin?" "'Knowledge puffeth up,'" they quote; "what men need is repentance, humility, faith, and love." And to all this every true educator will answer with a hearty "Amen." For none knows better than the educator the pitfalls of the intellect and the fallacies of mere knowledge. He knows very well, and is constantly asserting, that, though one knew all mysteries and had all knowledge, one would still remain an uneducated man unless he had love and faith and the real fruits of the spirit. There are those who adopt the phrases of religious education and miss its meaning. Apparently they endeavor only to secure in all persons a certain amount of information on religious sub-jects. They seem to hope to save the world by giving it lessons. It is not strange that all that seems foreign to the evangelistic spirit. It is foreign both to the evangelistic ideal and to educational method. Certainly if mere schooling is the best expression of the educational ideal then educa-tion holds forth no promise of accomplishing the world's redemption.

An attempt has already been made in this book to state the meaning of religious education, and especially to show how far it reaches beyond the lesson-learning processes. It has to do with lives, with persons, and with society.* Re-ligious education is not the substitution of knowledge about religion for a religious experience; but it is essentially a re-

* Summing up many definitions, one has characterized education as "a change of behavior through experience." See Mary E. Moxcey in *Girlhood and Character*, p. 47. For references to other definitions, see in Chapter III, at p. 28.

ligious experience. It is that developing experience of the whole universe that includes God and the infinite values, and under which persons grow to the completeness of their powers, abilities, and fitness in the universe. Paul spoke of it as growth from grace (*i. e.*, beauty of character) to grace, until we all come to the measure of the fulness of the stature of Christ. Does not Paul's phrase adequately express the evangelistic aim? Not the less does it express both the aim and the method of religious education.

EDUCATION VERSUS EVANGELISTISM

But, while we do insist that the apparent differences between education and evangelism in the church are founded on ignorance and naïve misapprehension, we must also insist that there are real and fundamental differences between the popular concepts of "salvation by evangelism" and the ideals of religious education. And because of the depth of these differences there is usually a very real difference between the church that is popularly known as an evangelistic church and the one that is loyal to the educational principles. The difference can be baldly stated as lying in the fact that the so-called evangelistic type expects the purpose of religion to be accomplished in men, in individuals, by a single experience known as conversion, while the educational type plans a programme of religious development which constantly touches all lives at every point and is never really completed. "Evangelism," as it is thus popularly conceived, consists in so moving on the consciences and emotions, and, rarely, on the minds of men, that this desired single experience is realized. All men are regarded as set off in two groups, the utterly lost or the wholly saved.

Those who have not been converted, and who have not accepted some particular theory of atonement, are lost— "without God and without hope in the world." Those who have "decided" or who "have been converted" (the active and the passive moods are popularly mixed here) are "saved," or "redeemed." Under these terms the programme of evangelism is very simple: by some means or another get every individual through this peak experience, and the immediate task is completed.

Whence comes this strange idea, strange at least to the good news of the kingdom of heaven? The trouble is not with the fundamental and proper conception of evangelism; it lies in the fact that the church has gradually allowed the professional "evangelist" to run away with evangelism, to engross all its meaning, and to centre and sum up all its aims and methods in his commonly lurid and abnormal practices. The churches have committed their direct and conscious evangelism to certain ones who pose as specialists. They have developed special methods, marked by strong idiosyncrasies. They have taught the churches to depend on their sporadic efforts. By the vagaries of their methods they have made evangelism an occasional and abnormal affair. Then they label themselves evangelists. At the best their methods are abnormal in the sense that a spanking is abnormal in family discipline—perhaps efficacious and necessary occasionally but always indicating something radically wrong not only in the child but in the family. At their worst their methods are abnormal as directly and consistently opposed to the laws of spiritual development. The present-day type of revivalism does not magnify religion; apparently it magnifies, first, the revivalist, and, second, a single emotional experience obtained at his meetings. It is a passing vogue in religious practice, popular because of its spectacular character, its advertising value, and its success in achieving what many churches regard as their very *raison d'être*, the addition of numbers to membership.*

Of course good comes of it; no one questions that spiritual good comes from the terrible European war. Religious good comes even from the highly mechanized, commercialized revival. It is, at least to many, a religious experience to be brought, by any means whatsoever, to think of their sins, to realize their meannesses, to think of death, to feel, under some emotional stress, that they give their lives to God. Doubtless many will join the church and for some of these the revival will mark the beginning of a developing religious experience. And all this might equally well be urged concerning some of the most terrible, bloody, and barbaric episodes in human history.

THE EVANGEL VERSUS REVIVALISM

The purpose of this chapter is not to denounce the revival, but to show how the evangelistic aim is accomplished by the educational processes. But it seems necessary, when so many, including leaders in the churches, show a tendency to depend almost wholly on the sporadic efforts of the revival-

* On the reaction from a current great revival and the retrograde effect on the churches, see the statistical study of the Welsh revival of 1905–6 in *The Church and the New Age*, by H. Carter, p. 34; and another study, "A Big Revival Two and One-Half Years After," by A. T. Morrison, in *The Christian Century* for December 21, 1911, being a study of the Springfield, Ill., revival. See also Dike, "A Study of New England Revivals," in *American Journal of Sociology*, vol. XV.

ist, to consider briefly the difference between revivalism and evangelism. Revivalism is not evangelism—at least it does not declare the Christian evangel. It substitutes for it the "good news" that men and women may in masses be swept by an emotional experience into aligning themselves with organized Christianity. That is its "evangel" to the churches; that is what makes it so attractive to religious people.* But the Christian evangel, "good news," is something quite different—it declares to all men that God loves them and would have them love him and love one another. It declares that God wills not the death of any sinner, but that all should turn to him and live with him and live as his family here. It speaks of salvation, completeness, wholeness. From Isaiah's glowing visions to the words of God's latest prophet it speaks of healing, redemption, freedom; of a world where men live with God, where sin no more works sorrow, injustice, pain, or oppression, but where men live in fulness of joy and life, a society redeemed and living according to the loving will of the Father of all. The evangel of the Gospels is the message of a new society, of brothers, of peace, of good will amongst men, of social healing and well-being, of a love that overcomes all things.

Now, this is the evangelism this age needs. It is the best antidote for evangelistism and revivalism. It is seen in the work of many churches. By teaching and training children, by guiding the lives of youth, by message and ministry to adults, they are declaring the good news that this is God's world and we may live the life of his will. The educational task of the church includes this work. By every means

* See the article by G. A. Coe, "Why Ministers Want Billy Sunday," in *The Congregationalist*, September 16, 1915.

possible it interprets life and the universe in the glad and
glowing terms of goodness, truth, and love. To youth who
seek a vision that makes life worth while, to all who, toil-
worn and harassed, seek life's meaning, the church brings the
good news of life. The pastor who so preaches that men
lift up their hearts in new courage, the teacher who so
teaches that childhood and youth give their days in high
devotion and service—these are doing the work of an
evangelist. They may well ignore the criticisms of the professional evangelist. But since his methods are so per-
sistently advocated they will do well to examine them with
some care.

Revivalism is not evangelism, because its message and
promise to men is one of *individualism;* it confirms them in
that individualistic morality and pietism which has made
possible our social disruption, hatred, and conflict. It offers
a legalistic alibi as to past iniquities and an inoculation to
their consequences. It teaches men to pat themselves on
the back, rejoicing that each has been snatched from the fate
of others. It teaches me to appreciate my own felicity in
being exempt from hell. It teaches this little me to ignore
the present ills—at least the ills of this world—because this
is but a threshold existence here: soon the door opens and I
enter my beautiful home where I can forget how wrong and
wicked this sad world is in all its suffering. Has revivalism
caused God's kingdom to come to this world or aided in giving to men what God wills for them? Has it shortened en-
slaving hours of labor, righted social wrongs, made the strong
love the weak, and the men of much goods help Lazarus,
not to crumbs from the table, but to wholeness and manhood? Has it rebuked the oppressor or delivered the mes-

sage of Isaiah, or of Amos, or of James, or of Jesus to the rich and the strong, and the sinners against the kingdom of God?

Revivalism is not evangelism, in that it substitutes a *single, partial experience* for that wholeness of life with which the gospel deals. The trouble is not that revivalism leads to an emotional experience; the trouble is that it leads to no more. It so magnifies and stresses this one experience as to make it a virtual cul-de-sac for the life.* It teaches that this moment of feeling, of high joy and pain, is religion—it is *the* religious experience, it makes one a Christian. Before it you were not, and now you wholly are. The entire interest turns about this ecstatic moment. The convert's mind goes back to it; he would repeat the experience over and over. Of course he finds that emotions never can be artificially revived, and so he makes the best of it and lives on the memory of that moment "in the tabernacle." Men need emotional experiences; that spring of conduct and will must be stimulated. But if emotional experiences are to have value the stimulus must stimulate to something; it must be a beginning and not a terminus. Most persons will have a memorable emotional experience on realizing that God loves them and on willing their love in turn. It is falling in love with God, with one ideally conceived in all beauty of person and character; but falling in love must go on to family living. That is the great evangel, not only that such a thrill of a new idea may come to one but that the idea may go on into its fulness of meaning, may grow and be increasingly realized all through life.

* On the dangers of the single experience, see Henry C. King, in *Personal and Ideal Elements in Education*, p. 162.

Revivalism often opposes evangelism by its low *moral ideals*. The task of the church in effecting the will of God in men and society will be seriously hampered wherever the debasing commercial features are manifest in revivalism. Its work will be retarded whenever it uses methods that are below the ethical and social standards of its day. It cannot lead the world forward if it turns backward to practise vulgarity and cheap sensationalism. It cannot lead men to the Saviour if it publicly repudiates the spirit of the gentle, loving Jesus. Nor can it make the spiritual really first in life if even so much as an appearance or suspicion of greed for money is prominent. On the contrary, such methods surely must constitute powerful forces for character degeneracy. Such methods speak so loud they will be remembered long after any message is forgotten. If our methods contradict the laws of life, if they lower the worker's self-respect and cause honorable men to hang their heads in apologetic shame, can we expect that the will of God will result? Can a permanent body of normally living Christians, growing in grace and in power to do God's will and cause it to be done, come from the exploitation of tricks and devices in crowd psychology?

Is this all that can be said for evangelism? No, there is the positive side. The educational programme calls for periods of special emphasis. It uses the power and advantage that come from gathering large numbers for a common purpose. It recognizes the need of wakening those who sleep. And it emphasizes the imperative necessity of stimulating lives by means of their emotions. Its purpose cannot be accomplished unless there are definite evangelistic plans, that is, plans to declare to men the good news of divine love. Men need, too, the most solemn declarations on the terrible losses they incur by rejecting such love. And these messages must be delivered under the most impressive conditions with every legitimate aid of emotional appeal. But all this is but part of an orderly conceived plan of meeting the needs of developing lives and the special needs of lives that have not developed normally.

For the normal person the religious experience is one of continuous development; but that development has its crises, its outstanding experiences. Then there are the many whose experiences are not normal, in whom the realization of the religious life must be quickened. They must be as those who are born again when they are already physically grown. The next chapter will deal with the special problem of reaching this group.

Any complete educational programme must include efforts to reach both the normal and the abnormal persons. The educational mission will reach out to every one. The special mission may be an educational project. It seeks to do in its sphere what special patriotic exercises in a school seek to do in the development of citizens. It is an educational project to make religion focal in the thought of a community by means of special meetings. The abuse of the evangelistic method, its occasional vulgar and debasing aspects, must not deter us from our full duty to those who need special stimulus and aid. Nor must we forget that such special aid is but the beginning of a continuous ministry of education.

The educator will not lose sight of the value of the mass appeal, nor of the special advantage of seasons and occasions which are set off and marked as specially for religious purposes. We have much to learn from revivalism. Remembering the errors and abuses which we have been emphasizing, is it not possible to use the advantages of the crowd and to direct the stimulus of great meetings and special occasions toward a splendid enthusiasm for righteousness? Just as all the quiet class-teaching in civics and ethics finds a splendid backing and stimulus in the great civic festival or in the patriotic meeting, we need to bring religion out into the area of larger enthusiasms and social feelings.

It is just as possible that large numbers shall together see the truth, feel helpful emotions, and develop real social religion as that they shall do the opposite. It is just as possible that large numbers shall feel the thrill of splendid hymns and the spiritual elevation of great music as that they shall be debauched by trash. The large number is the educator's opportunity. The present vogue of what seems to many to be so thoroughly harmful is our opportunity to discover and apply the right kinds of mass appeal in religion, the means of guiding large numbers into righteousness, or at least of giving them the right initial impulse. On no account must the educational church abandon a programme of evangelism. It must limit the field and redeem the methods of the present emphasis and it must apply itself to its own steady, normal programme of evangelism.

REFERENCES

JAMES, WILLIAM, *The Varieties of Religious Experience* (especially chap. X) (Longmans, 1902).

DAVENPORT, F. M., *Primitive Traits in Religious Revivals* (Macmillan, 1905).

DIKE, S. W., "A Study of New England Revivals" (*American Journal of Sociology*, vol. XV, 1909, p. 361).

KING, HENRY C., *Personal and Ideal Elements in Education* (Macmillan, 1904).

CHAPTER VIII

EDUCATIONAL EVANGELISM AND ADULTS

THE church with the educational ideal must not lose sight of the unquickened men and women in every community. For them it must devise the methods suited to their special needs. It will be loyal to the educational principle in the degree that its methods are actually based on their needs, on their natures, and on the religious aim in persons and in society.

If the programme of religious education could always reach all persons through all their lives, the number of these abnormal lives would be very small. But in fact the number is very large. They have been neglected. They must now be brought to know themselves as in God's family. This experience will come to them in varied ways, for some gradually, for others suddenly. For some it will come quietly, for others as a tremendous upheaval. But the large number of adults to whom religion is not a life experience constitute a real and serious part of the educational problem of the church.

THOSE WHO ARE WITHOUT

These words are being written in one of the largest cities of the South, in a city conscious of, and definitely proud of, its churches, in a section where in social custom and daily speech religion is as normal as patriotism is everywhere in this year of world fire and purging. In a few hours the church-bells will ring from many steeples and families will flock to their houses of worship. But, in spite of tradition and social usage, for every one in a church there will be three or four on the streets, riding to pleasure-resorts or seeking some form of diversion. That is the spectacle which presents a problem to every religious person to-day; it is the one which stirs churches to special evangelistic efforts.

It would be thoughtless to assume that non-attendance at church is an exact index to irreligion. Some are absent on account of their religion; their spiritual life does not strengthen itself in the ways that suit so many others. Many are absent because this day is the one opportunity they have for the freedom of the outdoors. But when all allowances have been made the fact remains that the greater number are without religious consciousness. There are multitudes, including many very intelligent persons, to whom religion is wholly foreign. Does the programme of religious education ignore these? If so, it is wofully deficient.

The problem is very real and vital. Even our emphasis on the importance of the child must help us to see this, for these unreached multitudes either are or soon will be the parents of the next generation. Unless their lives become consciously religious their children are most unlikely to have their full rights as religious persons; they will but repeat the shortened experiences of their parents.

A PROBLEM IN ATTENTION

The immediate problem is a very practical one, for the first step will be to get the attention of these people. This task religious education cannot ignore, for it is as truly the duty of education to begin any training that has been long neglected as it is to maintain training from the beginning. The difficulty is accentuated by our apparent lack of educational precedents in dealing with such a situation. It is further accentuated by our habit of thinking of education as confined to the young and restricted to formal instruction.

The task is, first, one of awakening intelligent interest. This interest may have many bases, such as quickened curiosity as to religion and its activities, awakened consciousness of personal deficiencies and needs, desire to share in the social life of the religious group, or desire better to discharge parental, civic, and social duties.

POSSIBLE PRECEDENTS

Perhaps we may discover a larger number of educational precedents than at first appear and a larger body of helpful experience than we have at first realized. Our problem is that of reaching adults, of arresting the passing crowd. At this time several nations are engaged in great and intensive programmes of adult education in national service. Men and women are being quickened to duties which, in increasing measure, are being conceived in terms wider than nationalism. The results in England and in North America are familiar to all. While many of the methods are not educationally sound and many are not at all applicable to the problem of religion, there are still valuable lessons to be learned from this educational endeavor. Generally speaking, the methods are those used in well-conceived advertising campaigns. Much modern advertising is carefully based on scientific principles determined by psychological investigations. The principles we would follow must have this common basis.

First: Attention is secured by appeals which make contacts with the *present thinking and experience* of adults. This is a primary principle of teaching. To lead the learner every teacher must begin his teaching where the learner now is in thought and feeling. Contacts are made through language. For this popular teaching of adults simple, non-technical language is used. Whether it be posters or editorials or the presentation of information it is in the language of the people. But note that experience has indicated that it does not pay to use slang. An examination of the many forms of material used will show a steady tendency increasingly to respect both the taste and the intelligence of even that mythical creature, the man on the street. Contacts are made through experience. Appeals are based on present interests. They are put into terms of the present-day facts of our own lives. Certainly the religious teacher can profit by that lesson. When religion comes to men so as to show its realities in their own lives, its place in their homes and daily affairs, they receive it gladly. So often campaigns that otherwise are conceived on the basis of much advertising wisdom fail because they present only ideas of another world; even where their language is not theological their thought is unreal—outside of human, common experience.

Second: The great educational efforts to win adult attention use a *variety of avenues*. They are addressed to the eye as well as to the ear. They present themselves in forms of artistic beauty. They appeal, through the eye, not only by posters but also by impressive symbols. Has the church used fully the power of symbols presented to the public? There is a vast difference between a symbol of religion which is regarded as possessed of some supernatural power and a symbol which serves as a key to associations of memory or of aspiration. The symbol is a form of language. In small compass it may speak a message; it may waken memories; it may embody long historical associations, all of which may stir the imagination and the feelings as no printed words could do. Surely every educator ought to use every form of language which can be understood by those whom he would educate.

Third: Present-day adult education uses the stimulus of the *pageant*. The sense of civic duty is quickened by pageants showing the past history, and, in allegorical form, the future promise of the civic life. Regiments march through the city streets for the sake of the people on the sidewalks. The spectacle speaks of more than a present situation; it brings to minds and wills the force of historical and ideal associations. A pageant like "The Mission Play" given in California creates a new appreciation of the part that one church played in the early life of the Pacific coast; but it also creates a sense of the reality of the religious organization in all life.

Fourth: One of the most potent means by which attention is enlisted and personal loyalty is awakened is that of *service*. One root of our quickened patriotism is the sense of a common helpful life in which we share and for which we are grateful. Ministry wins men. It is effective largely in the degree that it looks for no return, when it is unconscious of its power to win. Every service the church renders is an exposition of its worth and an appeal to the co-operation of all right-minded persons. This is not a plea for any plan of purchasing people by soup or by any form of service.

It is simply an insistence on the power of the practical message of service. Even the indifferent know love when it reaches them in helpful ways. This is teaching by the most direct means. It declares the gospel of divine love by a demonstration of human brotherhood at work. There is no rebuttal of its arguments. It educates just as the continuous ministry of sacrifice in the family educates all whom it reaches.

Fifth: These appeals are designed to lead to simple steps of *action*. They are addressed to beginnings. They present no long arguments and they prescribe nothing beyond the next and the feasible action. This is illustrated in much good advertising. One is urged to do the next thing. This is not guile; this is good educational sense. Teaching is always by steps. It is possible to lead only from what we now experience into what we can see just before us. That step taken, the next one appears.

Sixth: The steps are *practical*. Experience reveals fully their meanings. The deed precedes the doctrine. We are still commonly attempting to invert that process in religious teaching. But the great Teacher won men by calling them to walk with him, to do the next, simple thing. But it is not only a practical and simple step that is to be taken; it must have reality and meaning. Joining a church might seem to be a simple step; but it will not be taken unless it is seen as a worth-while, meaningful one. Almost all who have had experience in work in the church will recall persons who have come into its life through an invitation to share, at some point of practical need, in its work. The first act has been the beginning of practical training in the religious life. Those who participate learn that life by liv-

ing it. The lessons may be unconscious; they will be spoiled
if morals are attached to them. Let each one discover for
himself the significance of these steps.

Seventh: Adult attention is won by *appeals of a high
character.* The successful posters are those which somehow brace our idealism even before they compel our action.
They command our respect and they seem to say: "We respect you, we believe in your higher motives." At least in
the United States, and doubtless everywhere else, more men
worth winning have been won by appeals to ideal interests
than by appeals to self-interest. Fear seems to have failed
as a motive here. One cannot meet the college boys who
have gone first to the front without getting a new measure
of faith in their idealism, nor without realizing that, under
the protective coloring of their cynicism and indifference,
lie keys that rightly touched give out the music of splendid
ideals. One must believe in men to win them. The best
appears only when the best is called.

EDUCATIONAL RESPONSIBILITY FOR THE UNCHURCHED

Is it not high time, recognizing the needs of the large
numbers of unawakened persons, to give more careful attention to this problem than we have yet given? Have we not
too readily adopted and solely depended upon methods
which have no better basis than guesses and hopes? We
have discovered our plans by accident or we have adopted
them upon assumptions. It is the duty of the church to use
in this high task all that can be learned from educational
science. The psychology of the adult is the clue to the adult
life. We cannot win these lives save as we obey the laws of
life. Then we must lay tribute to all educational experience

wherever it may be found, not only in colleges and schools but in the great experiments in advertising and in the present educational propaganda for patriotic service.

In every church there might well be a group to whom this problem is committed as a special interest. It need not be a committee or board, publicly announced; but the pastor might select those persons who could appreciate the problem and who would be likely to study it with him. They would find it an exceedingly interesting one. It would lead into the history of revivals, into the history and present practice of advertising, into the study of political campaigns, and, most important of all, into the study of the minds and wills of men and women. Such a group would be able to feel that they were facing one of the most difficult and most neglected tasks of the church, that they were learning God's ways of working, that they were embarked on a truly splendid enterprise.*

Their task would be in the most exact sense educational. They would be concerned with the quickening of lives, with the beginnings of that development in life and character which is the aim of religious education in the church.

This chapter has emphasized beginnings for adults; it has attempted to face the special problem of arresting and enlisting the attention of the indifferent. But beginnings are only worth while when they are seen as only beginnings. These are some of the means of securing attention; the lesson of life must follow. For adults who begin their lessons so late in life there is needed special training.

Whenever in any community special concentrations of

* This committee might make a collection of the posters used in the recruiting, Red Cross, Liberty Loan, and Y. M. C. A. campaigns.

religious emphasis have succeeded in quickening numbers of persons who have been out of all relations to the programmes of the churches, these persons constitute a peculiar problem in religious education. Their training in the life of a religious society has been, frequently, wholly neglected or avoided. The assumption that their striking religious experiences in the special meetings will make up for this deficiency is not a valid one. Whatever their theoretical standing may be, practically they are novices in the religious society. They are initiates and must be trained in its life. Therefore the educational programme must make special provision for these newly awakened ones.

Courses of study for the adult fruits of special evangelism —as contrasted with the results of the steady evangelism going on through the normal programme of religious training —should be more than rapid-survey courses designed to do quickly that which normally would take years. They should be based upon the adult's needs. They would include knowledge of the history of faith and of the church, the meaning of religion in the life of to-day, the special religious problems of thought, and, especially, carefully arranged training in the practice of the every-day religious life and service in the church and in the world.

REFERENCES

Scott, W. D., *Psychology of Advertising* (Small, 1906).

McGarrah, A. F., *A Modern Church Program* (Revell, 1915).

McDowell, W. F., *Good Ministers of Jesus Christ*, lecture V (Abingdon Press, 1917).

Men and Religious Messages, vol. VII, secs. 7–9 (Association Press, 1912).

The Sunday School Executive (monthly, D. C. Cook) publishes excellent examples of posters.

CHAPTER IX

THE EDUCATIONAL EVANGEL

HAS the educational ideal any further significance or place in the programme of evangelism? Holding and declaring the Christian good news, how does the church use the educational method? A full answer would be a statement of the whole programme of the church. By all means that are right it teaches; it seeks to make all men know the good news of the love of God and it stimulates, directs, and trains them into the realization in their own lives and in the social whole of all that the good news means. The educational method seeks to realize the full evangelistic message.

Let all who believe in the educational programme in the church insist on its evangelistic validity and value. Let them keep constantly in mind the evangelistic aim. Let them answer—by their religious devotion to lives, to persons, to the divine ideal for men and for society—the superficial sneer against education as a merely academic affair. The church as an educator is dealing with matters too vital ever to allow herself to become merely an academic institution: she is a life-growing institution, and, as a society, she is more than an institution; she is a life-growing organism. All her programme of education has the evangelistic aim, is moved into action by the evangelistic motive, and is determined by the evangelistic principle of dealing with men as the children of God.

Is there, then, any difference between evangelism and

education? It has been suggested that there are certain vast differences between popular evangelism and religious education, but the nature of these essential differences can be seen best by looking with a little care at the distinctive features of the educational ideal and programme in the church so far as they relate to the evangelistic aim. This will also help to answer the question, How can the evangelistic church use the educational method?

LIFE, THE EVANGELISTIC AIM

The first characteristic of the education ideal in a church is a consciousness of *vital* processes. Education deals with living beings. It is vital, not mechanical, statistical, nor institutional. Living beings are its materials, life is its method, and living persons its essential mechanism. Its aim is to modify and develop lives. Ideas, doctrines, traditions, philosophies are but tools. It does not work for the sake of "the truth," that is, for any special body of facts. It seeks the truth in order that truth may serve. Truth has no value at all save in relation to people, save as it passes over into reality through action and becomes life. A church does not fulfil its purpose by acting as a reservoir for truth; it sends truth gushing out through the channels of life, purifying, invigorating, and serving men. It is not called to mount guard over a set of statements called "the truth," set off in a vault or a glass case. Truths thus sequestrated are dead. It causes truth to flame—to burn and warm and warn. It causes truth to set men's hearts and brains afire, to change men's minds and thus to change the world. Its relation to truth is that of the workman who holds a fine tool; he must master it and make it useful.

So the church can know whether her work is being done, not by whether certain doctrines are preserved but by whether men are changed, by what takes place in lives. Hers is a garden where grow the sons of men; she deals not with the dead past, not with organization and tradition, but with lives first, lives which she will develop by the use of every appropriate means. So that the educational ideal insists on one simple and very essential element of evangelism; it is directed to persons. It goes farther, it seeks the salvation of persons; it seeks their realization of the divine ideal.

This vital function in religious education has to do with *lives as wholes,* in contrast to the notion of dealing with separate parts, "hearts," "souls," and minds. The life is not separable into either faculties or "belts." A man cannot be saved in his affections and remain unsaved, diseased and filthy, in mind or imagination. The church is not a specialized institution to deal with souls while the school deals with minds and the rest of organized society cares for bodies. The person acts as a whole; he is what all his being feels and knows and does. To be saved his whole self must be saved. Salvation by a single mental act or an emotional experience cannot complete the work of growing this person to the fulness of the divine ideal. Here, in this view of life, is one great and easily seen difference between the current evangelistic emphasis and the educational ideal. The former touches life only at the point of a single experience, and usually only through one activity of the person; the latter seeks by continuous process always to involve all the activities and powers. The former seeks the acceptance of one aspect of truth; the latter seeks a life that steadily moves forward, in growing light of truth, in growing love of

God, in growing beauty of life and harmony with all lives. The educational ideal emphasizes the breadth of the true evangelistic appeal.

THE NOTE OF REALITY

This vital function has to do with *real lives*. In the school and college modern education has been coming out of the closet of antiquities into the workshop and ways of life; we are learning to see education not only as a process for life but as a process *through* the experience of life. Through the realities of living we really find life. So in the church there is a consciousness of dealing with reality, with this immediate present experience as the very school through which larger life is realized. The educational programme of such a church consists in much more than courses in the philosophy and history and literature of religion. It is a programme of experience. It demonstrates the educational principle that "if any man will do His will he shall know of the doctrine." Education shares the pragmatic note of modern social evangelism.

This principle of reality is of central importance. It shows the only way that religion becomes real in life. Nothing is real until it is realized, until in some way it enters vitally into experience. We have discarded some ideals in education; the pale bookworm and the erudite delver in dead dust are no longer the typical products of education. But the present programme of religious education is still cramped by vestiges of the informational ideal; for many the favorite word is "curricula"; their tools are books and their goals examinations. Modern education has as its motto the words of Jesus: "I am come that they might have life and that they might have it more abundantly."

Then, too, the principle of reality dominates method in religious education. As Carlyle said, "Men do not become saints in their sleep"; it matters not whether they try the process in pews or dreaming through the glories of the past. Lives develop when they are in activity, when experience is functioning. True, we need classrooms and courses of study; they are the machinery and the agencies which stimulate and guide activity. But somehow we must make sure that all teaching goes over into experience, that all becomes real in the life of the learner. No one knows the worth of the soul until, as the old evangelistic phrase had it, he "works for souls." The work may be done in new ways to-day, as well as in some old ways; but it must be done not only for the sake of the work but also for the sake of the worker.

The vital function has to do with *growing lives*. Because they are the lives of persons, under personal relations, living through experience, they must grow. Here is no static aim, but a dynamic and therefore a developing one. Such a life does not reach fulness in some heated moment; growth goes on through all the days. It follows One who grew in wisdom and stature. Here again is readily seen the distinction between the popular evangelistic idea and the educational ideal. But one will also see the identity between this ideal and the message so frequently emphasized in the New Testament. The evangel declares that men may grow in grace, that lives must become steadily more Godlike.

FAITH IN LAW

Very closely connected is the next great vital principle: these *growing lives develop in an orderly manner, under law.* We accept the universality of law in all other realms of life.

Is it possible we are in a universe that mocks us by having a law for the life of the squash and none for the soul, that here apples grow according to discoverable laws but persons must be left to chance, to accident, or to laws that no man may know? The faith of the educational ideal holds that it is possible to know how people do grow as religious persons, how they do develop Godward. It holds that, knowing this, it is possible to order and control the processes toward the desired result. It is marked by patient endeavor to know the laws of life, this whole life, and to obey them. This is the attitude of true reverence. Here is where men walk truly with unshod feet. To ignore the laws of life is to walk roughshod, in blatant assumption of the superiority of our ignorance and our guesses over God's eternal truth. The educator is ever a learner; he seeks to read the book of life and to him all its pages are sacred. That willingness to learn everywhere, the avoidance of the scoffer's seat wherever found, is the mark of the scientific mind.

The vital principle sees life *growing always*. In life growth of some sort must be continuous in some form. Because here we are working with the whole of real persons, we must work with the whole of their experience, with the full range of their lives. This implies not only the range of interests but all the range of time and experience. This is the logic of Horace Bushnell's principle of "Christian Nurture." *
It makes little difference what your theological views may be in regard to the "status" of the little child; the fact remains that the child is alive and growing and becoming. To direct the development of this person we must deal with him in all stages of his becoming. That holds good as far as

* Revised edition, published by Charles Scribner's Sons, 1917.

we can see and as far as we can reach. Much current practice in religion apparently hopes to grow a full life by beginning when it is half-spent. Its emphasis is on a midway event called conversion. Education recognizes the tremendous importance of the conversion experience, but it also recognizes that this is determined by what has gone before. It sees all experience, before and after, as part of the whole process of a growing life.

Many of us heartily believe that the youngest child is at least as much the object of the Infinite affection as any grown man, or any person, whatever his theological status may be. Religion is such an experience in life that we never can find the time when, so long as consciousness is discoverable to us, the experience may not function in some way. It is never too early to be religious, that is, to feel and think, to the best of our abilities, of life as having spiritual value. It is never too early to pray, to aspire, to think of God in the beauty and joy and love of the world. It is never too soon for the life to begin to grow, to gain its powers, acquire its habits, and find its fulness. But it is important to remember that if religion is real to a child it will be a child's religion; the form of expression will be consonant with the stage of development.

Religious education does not wait for the development of some contrary experience; it does not wait for wandering in order to make "returning" real. It does not assume the normality of the rake's progress in every life, nor predicate the consciousness of being the real child of God upon a prodigal's experience. The evangel of religious education is that men already have in them all the possibilities of the religious life, and that the really normal experience would be that no child should ever think of himself, either in childhood or later, as any other than God's child, nor ever live in any other way.*

Most faith in "infant damnation" applies only to the neighbor's children; our doubts about children belonging to God do not affect our attitude to our own children. From their first breaths we pray that they may be his children. We assume in all our dealings with them that they really are his children. We want them to grow up always so thinking, and looking out always on the world as seen through such a thought, as seen as the world of his great love. Pragmatically parenthood overcomes all other polemics when we look at a little one.† Thus the educational ideal includes the message of good news concerning the children, "the least of these little ones."

So the church regards the children. No matter what pretensions she may make of an educational programme the vital test is just here: What does she do for the children? Have they a real place in her life? Does her programme mean that she cares for the whole of lives, and, most of all, does it mean that her best endeavors are centred on their growth at the time when growth most effectively and potentially takes place? Does she set the child in the midst?

EPOCHAL EXPERIENCES

The educational ideal, then, sees religion as a life experience—always possible in some way, doubtless always present

---

* See *The Moral Condition and Development of the Child*, by W. A. Wright (Jennings and Graham, 75 cents).

† See *Preservation vs. Rescue of the Child*, by John T. McFarland, pamphlet (Eaton & Mains).

in some way. It sees the programme of religion as bringing every life steadily forward, all through its experiences, from the earliest beginning through all its phases into all its fulness. Of course it does not dream that such a development is always on a serene, unvarying level. To do so would be to ignore what we know of the laws under which life grows. It recognizes crises, great epochal points. There is a moment when the apple that has been growing so long bursts its spring sheath and a glowing flower breaks forth; the whole hillside flames with the tender glory. That is an orderly step toward the ripe apple. There is, for at least many lives, a time when consciousness breaks forth on a new world; the life finds itself, its fellows, its world, and its God. It is a wonderful experience; there may never be anything else like it, but it is all a part of the normal development of the person. Conversion is a crisis; but a crisis is only a part of a process, a progress.*

Religious education also recognizes that all it may learn about the laws of life is but the discovery of God, that, just as the man who grows the apples knows that the whole universe grows them with him, so we who would grow lives are not so blinded with pride of learning as to imagine that we work alone, or to think that all we do is comparable to all that is being done. The educator is only the husbandman. God works, but the hand of the husbandman is absolutely essential; God does not cause orchards to be without it. And the husbandman's knowledge is absolutely essential; nature will not remedy his mistakes or make up for his

* On the normality of the conversion experience, see *The Psychology of Religion*, by E. D. Starbuck (1899), and compare chap. X of *The Psychology of Religion*, by G. A. Coe (1916). See also James's *Varieties of Religious Experience*, 1902, lectures IX and X.

ignorance. The more we realize the worth of a person the greater will be our reverence for the processes of developing lives, the more patiently will we seek to know the laws of lives and the greater will be our obedience to them. The very principle of vitality, of dealing with lives, makes religious education religious; it is a serious endeavor to take our right part in the spiritual order and plan of the universe.

So the educational ideal holds the faith that the evangelistic aim of religious persons in a religious society is normally achieved by the essentially religious process of the growth of lives toward Godlikeness. Its method is continuous, according to law, comprehending all life's experiences and possibilities, knowing no fixed goal, but moving forward into newer and larger fulness of life. It realizes the promise of an evangel by revealing the manner in which that promise may be fulfilled. It shows how we learn to live the life of love in the divine family. It trains us to live that life increasingly and habitually. It prepares us to do the work by which the promise of a divine social order is to be realized. It is the method by which the message of evangelism is fulfilled.

REFERENCES

BUSHNELL, HORACE, *Christian Nurture* (Scribners, revised edition, 1917).

MCKINLEY, C. E., *Educational Evangelism* (Pilgrim Press, 1905).

HARDY, E. N., *The Churches and Educated Men* (Pilgrim Press, 1904).

COE, GEORGE A., *The Psychology of Religion* (in particular chap. X) (University of Chicago Press, 1916).

CONDE, BERTHA, *The Human Element in the Making of a Christian* (Scribners, 1917).

CHAPTER X

THE WORLD–WIDE PROGRAMME

THE evangel of the church has one peculiarly thrilling aspect; it is world-embracing. The evangelistic aim is a world society united in the relations of a single family under the divine fatherhood. No church can be loyal to that aim so long as it thinks in purely local terms. No educational programme can be complete so long as it is only parochial. What a wonderful dream, an imperial vision—the picture of a world society—to be held by a small sect of lowly men and women in the early centuries! But to-day it is fast coming to full realization, not alone through the ministry of the churches but by the movements of commerce, industry, and politics.

The church of to-day is part of a world society. The old order of local and national isolation has passed; the new dawns with a world consciousness. The polarization of population in the cities has developed new habits of social living. Commerce and industry, serving and laying tribute on all parts of the world, have made each man increasingly dependent on all others. There has been a like exchange and interplay of thought throughout the world. We are thinking in unity. The weaving of a vast, intricate, and efficient system of communication by rapid transit, telephones, rural mail-delivery, and wireless has created a nervous system for all mankind that gives us a common life.

No parts of the world are any longer remote.   No part can say to another: "I have no need of thee."*

WORLD–NEIGHBORING

Through the experiences of the opening decades of the twentieth century we have a new world-neighboring.   The bands of copper and steel had bound the world with new ties and made us know one another, but the furnace of a world at war fused all together, and knowledge deepened into sympathy.   New nerves have ramified through the body of the world life, nerves of intense and high feeling.   We have become one in a blood bond.   The foreigner and foreign things are no more; the dwellers in the remotest places are much more familiar to us than the people of the next-door nation were when we were children.   In a few short years we passed from nationalism to internationalism, and then to world thought and life.

The church does not stand apart from such great changes. A social revolution like this profoundly affects an institution so essentially social.   Such an extension of neighboring, such an enriching of the points of vital contact must mean a greatly widened horizon.   It must involve new concepts, new duties.   Now that we have come to that world consciousness which is so marvellous a fact in the mind of Jesus, we must come more completely to his sense of the world as the object of divine love and the field of redemption. Will not such an extension of social vision lead away from individualism in religion and toward the social vision of the salvation of the whole human order?

* On the spiritual significance of these changes, see Henry C. King, *Moral and Religious Challenge of Our Times.*

The current changes in the social order immediately affect one part of the work of the church. They have already robbed "home missions" of its peculiar romantic flavor, for the "wild West" is no more and the desert places begin to blossom as the rose. They have taken away altogether the former significance of the phrase "foreign missions," for in a world society, where there are no foreigners, there can be no foreign missions. The same people are there, and they have not all changed; but we have changed; we see them with new eyes. They do not need us less; they can claim us more. They are foreign to us no longer; they are actually—not in hymn-book phrase alone —of our family. Whatever is done for the men and women of India, Korea, China, Africa can no longer be regarded as addenda to the normal activities and programme of the church. They are not optional responsibilities, so many fifth wheels of which we are childishly proud. All are part of the necessary programme of the church, a programme which grows out of the purpose of realizing religious character and religious conditions in life. They rise out of the fact that this social institution, the church, must work in the whole range of its social setting.

A PROGRAMME OF WORLD EDUCATION

For her own educational work at home the church must reach out to all the world. In order that the local church may carry out its programme of bringing the lives of its own people to fulness it must insure for them *normal contacts with their whole environment.* The breadth and strength of every life depends on the variety and reality of its contacts. A man of narrow, restricted interests cannot but be a small

man. The farther one looks and reaches the farther he
lives. The larger the spiritual family of which we are a part
the richer grows our own spiritual life. It is outreach that
enlarges the heart. So also into every life there flow new
treasures of knowledge and new riches of feeling and interest from each new contact that it makes with a wider
world.

The training of Christian character requires the experiences of *enlarging social living*. We have to learn to live in
a larger family. Our relation to the far-away peoples is not
that of the smug, satisfied, saved ones at home who benevo-
lently dole out doctrine or dollars to the lost in darkness.
It is closer and simpler; it rises out of the fact that we who
live so close together have to learn the art of living together.
Surely the first step in that art is sharing life together.
The true missionary spirit and programme simply makes the
whole world our great schoolroom of the spiritual life. Here
we teach others to live toward Christ only as we live Christly
toward them.

The missionary programme *changes our own minds*. We
will not go far toward making the world the society of God
unless we can take the notion of the foreign out of all our
relations to others. Somehow we must lose the sense of
remoteness and of artificial relations instituted and maintained by our altruism. The relations are inevitable and
essential; we cannot escape from the other man in this
world order. And essentially he is not an inferior; he is a
family fellow. He may be different, but he lives by the
same powers of life; he is a person and he is bound up with
us in this bundle of the world's life. The educational task
of the church is no longer that of training young people to

give a dollar where they used, with difficulty, to divert a penny from its candy destination. It is no longer a programme of winning volunteers by either the appeal of the romantic in date-palms, jungles, and jinrikishas, or the appeal of the pathetic lot of those without the pale. It is the task of training us all to live in this new great family and so to bear ourselves in all things to all that all men shall rejoice in owning the one Father.

The programme of missionary education, then, in the church, from the very beginning in every life, will seek to develop the simple consciousness of living in *one common social order* that embraces all men. It will, by every means in its power, wipe out the notion of the foreigner, break down and cast out race prejudice, and build up and make common and natural the thought of real, effective brotherhood. It will cease to base appeals for missionary giving and effort on the motive of the far, remote, and unknown, and base them on the near, on the real, social propinquity of all men to ourselves, on the essentially common life we live. It will be directed, first, to the training of motives and concepts of life. This it will accomplish by the development of habits —habits of speech, of action, of thought. It will bring again the whole world into the region of normal religious thinking. We shall cease to think of this as the one God-favored land, of which the Almighty is especially proud. It will save us from national pharisaism.

NEIGHBORING BY KNOWING

The programme of missionary education will make the remote near and real in just the same way that the unknown in geography and ethnology has become familiar to us in

all other affairs. Travel, lectures, pictures, and means of
communication have so disclosed life everywhere that were
we unexpectedly dropped on the plaza of St. Mark's or before the sweep of the harbor at Nagasaki we should know
our surroundings. This means more than that architec-
tural marvels and natural beauties have become familiar;
it means that we have learned to know people as they live
everywhere. When we have thus learned that people are
people everywhere we have taken an exceedingly important
step toward world thinking and feeling. So missionary
education by the travel-picture method is not a whet-
ting of generosity by appeals to curiosity or to pity; it
is education into the normality of the common life of all,
into deeper, more constant and real sympathy with all
life.*

Such education broadens out, even on the plane of knowledge, in many different ways. It will mean such a study of
the development and the romance of missions as shall make
us see how the gospel has been wiping out walls of partition,
paving the way for great social changes, and making this a
new world. It brings to the young the heroes of modern
religion. Actually knowing the lives of the great leaders
will effect a new realization of the eternal law that life can
be given to the world only by the laying down of life. It
will help us to see what life in this world order must cost
us if we are to live as religious men. Thus to think of the
continuous, unending sacrifice which love offers up for life
is to acquire the habit of thinking of all life in like terms.

* For the materials of such study, see particularly the numerous
publications of The Missionary Education Movement, and especially
Diffendorfer's *Missionary Education in the Home and School.*

KNOWING THE WORLD LIFE

Missionary education must also mean for all thoughtful persons a thorough understanding of the elements of our world problems. Without this there is little hope of their solution. To-day we are actually engaged in shaping a new social order, in making a new world. Such a task we cannot lightly attempt; if it has any reality it calls us to a thorough understanding of all its factors. It will require some knowledge of the political life, the social customs, the traditions, and the religious ideals and forces of all the parts of this human family. We shall do more than know how people cook and eat and build houses. If we are to live with them we will want to know how they think, how their minds work, what hopes they fashion in the brain.

Some will say that this large programme calls for more study than any one can give to-day, but there is nothing this age needs more than a large programme. We are most of us so busy because we are trying to do so large a number of insignificant things; we have no great, overwhelming values that force all other things into their relative places. A few people are supremely happy because life does mean for them so many tremendous things. The man with the world on his heart and in his mind is happier by far than any to whom it is known as but a plaything. To have such a sense of the reality of this world problem will keep it ever before us, will make us study its elements, work for the least grain of its solution, and hold ever the hope of the new world. It will make new men of us all. It will set the world in our hearts. It will thus broaden, deepen, and heighten our very selves. It will give us what Jesus had—a world for which to live.

The programme of education in the missionary spirit in the church will be also a programme of actual instruction and training in the ways of world living. At present we teach the young that God loved the world, but we do not teach them how to love it and still less how to live in it. The one is impossible without the other. You cannot live in this world unless you love it, and you cannot love it until you really live in it. Out of the proper emphasis on the duty of the church definitely to teach the art of actual Christian living, of the right life in the family, on the streets, in the school, on the playground, and in all relations, grows the farther and wider one of teaching the art of living the world life. Supposing, to be very specific, instead of spending years tracing the wanderings of the Hebrews, we should actually face the problem of walking our ways of life with the modern Hebrews. No one is so blind as not to see that problem. Gentile and Jew do not always agree. In the young, especially in public school and other schools, the bitterness of race prejudice grows apace. We all know it is there; we hear it in sneering phrase and see it in social ostracism. But what does the church school do about it? How many teachers help the child to see the Christian's duty toward the Jewish child? How many deliberately set out to train Christian children to be gentle and Christlike to their Jewish playmates? If we think that the situation is insoluble we acknowledge that the world order of the kingdom of God is impossible. If we think we can shut our eyes to the situation, or can afford to hate any people, we deny the Teacher of human love, we steadily augment the shame that our present attitude calls on his head. It is not an easy question but, if ever we are to realize the spirit and aim of world missions we too must begin at Jerusalem. It is so much easier to feel brotherly to a mud-caked African who stays in Africa than to many a representative of another race who comes into our city block. Education in the missionary programme of the church will surely mean training in Christian living with all mankind.*

Out of such a programme of training to live the world life, to develop the world sympathy and habit of thought, grows an intelligent, enthusiastic support of all that operates to realize here the God-willed world order of one divine family. Men and women no longer support this or that home or foreign missionary society as such; they see the society as a tool to be used, developed, or scrapped according to its efficiency in realizing the great purpose. They support a programme. They are not interested in missionary operations as ends in themselves but as means, as parts of the machinery that accomplishes a magnificent end, and therefore their interest is the greater in the means because the end is so great. They cease to be blind and therefore stingy givers; they support intelligently a world work and they will know and cannot be misled as to whether the machinery is doing the work or not.

It is not strange that the missionary programme is a big problem in the church to-day. Emphasis on the machinery, the societies and missionaries, has often magnified them

* On the problem in the United States, see *The New Immigration*, by Peter Roberts, 1912.

into ends.   Emphasis on their support has often obscured the
tremendous values in their results.   And when we think
of the societies as ends we become suspicious of their value.
But in the light of a magnificent world aim we are able to
judge calmly and rightly whether the present methods are
wise, whether they are the ones by which the Christian
world society is to be realized.   In the light of that aim we
ought to help youth to understand the work of the modern
societies.   They would find in many of their present-day
programmes guidance on the problems of the church at home.
In many instances the work in India, in China, and other
lands is demonstrating the real function of a church.   Problems are being solved there on which we are still debating
here.   The solutions have come because the leaders have
seen the world vision and have had the courage to follow it.
A knowledge of the realities of present-day missions is a valuable part of training for home work.   It further strengthens
faith in the educational programme.   The great progress of
work abroad has been seen in emphasis upon educational
methods.   Some day the church at home will learn from the
church abroad.

The very experience of a world programme has had a remarkable effect on the workers abroad.   It has taught them
to place first the larger values.   It has set in the foreground
the ultimate purpose of developing lives into a religious
society.   By that aim every method must be tested.   Toward
that aim all our training should be directed.   Religious education includes a programme based on the vision of the
world coming into the common family life of God—a vision
that gives a new conscience, a new motive, and a new
method.

Missionary education, then, is simply a phase of religious education.   It is essential to complete training in Christian living.   Its aim is much more significant than the development of support for missionary enterprises;   it seeks to develop persons who fully live the world life in a religious spirit.   It accomplishes its special purposes by instruction designed to reveal our religious relations to life everywhere in the world and by training in discharging the duties of those relationships.   It uses all those organized agencies which have been created to develop and guide the churches in living the world life, and directs an intelligent participation in their work as part of its plan of training.

REFERENCES

BEARD, FREDERICA, " Graded Missionary Education in the Church School " (*American Baptist*, 1917).

CARVER, W. O., *Missions and Modern Thought* (Macmillan, 1910).

DIFFENDORFER, R. E., *Missionary Education in Home and School* (Abingdon, 1917).

DOUGLASS, H. P., *The New Home Missions* (Missionary Education Movement, 1914).

FAUNCE, W. H. P., *Social Aspects of Foreign Missions* (Missionary Education Movement, 1914).

MOTT, JOHN R., *The Pastor and Modern Missions* (Student Volunteer Movement, 1904).

Education in Relation to the Christianization of National Life, vol. III of Report of Edinburgh Conference, 1910 (Revell).

CHAPTER XI

THE SOCIAL LIFE

Four great educational opportunities are offered to the church in what is loosely called its social life: (1) the social grouping of persons permits of training in social relations; (2) it affords opportunities for the growth of group loyalties; (3) it facilitates organization for service; and (4) it furnishes conditions for helpful social worship. Since the last of these is considered in the section on "Worship," we can confine ourselves to the church as a school of the social life and as a community that develops group loyalties.

THE SCHOOL OF A SOCIETY

Essentially a school is a social group. It can perform its primary work of instruction only as it gathers lives in groups. Even for the purposes of imparting information and training in habits it must organize persons not as individuals but as groups. But every teacher knows, what so many parents do not see, that the school educates, not alone by instruction, but still more by associating lives together in the habits of living. There is no schooling where this is not done. A schoolroom is more than a child plus a lesson plus a teacher; it is rather many children feeling a common aim, under the cumulative power of their many lives, plus the stimulus of a purpose and a guide.*

* On the school as a social organization, see Irving King, in *Social Aspects of Education*, 1912, particularly chaps. I to IV; and John Dewey, *School and Society*, 1910.

In school children learn the larger social life through their smaller social group. Education is developing persons by the experiences of the larger life. Children are learning to live in their communities, getting the art of social living by social living. It is a familiar truism that they learn more on the playground than at their desks; in the former the social group is larger, has a wider range of free activity, depends on its own guidance and initiative, and develops more intense activity.

For purposes of education two people are much more than one plus one; they are the sum of all the social feelings, co-operations, stimuli that develop as mind and personality act and react one on another. The cumulative process of increasing power goes on in a progressive ratio as the number increases. It is true that if one shall chase a thousand, two shall put ten thousand to flight. The group consists of persons doing at least two things: adjusting themselves one to another, each to all and all to each, and stimulating each other, as knowledge, feeling, and will grow in each and are shared by all until the feeling develops cumulatively to a mass that moves each one. This is more than a matter of addition or accretion. The crowd really creates a new life.

We all know that four people always do the same thing in unison much more easily, effectively, and usually more pleasurably, than the same four doing the same thing independently. Have we considered how that simple fact may be used in the church for the development of characters and usefulness? The minister often tends to think of a congregation of largely unrelated persons. He is likely to measure his work in terms of so many individuals affected in cer-

tain ways. He seldom considers, in bringing a group together, in what ways—under the principles of human thinking, feeling, and willing—the forces that are in the group,
and not in the individuals, may be used. He does not have
a working plan, based on the laws of persons and society,
which will determine his method with his several groups or
with his entire group.

There are few fields of knowledge more essential to the
minister of the church than that of social psychology, and
few more helpful and fruitful, provided, of course, the subject
be based upon an understanding of the simple, elementary
principles of general psychology. He deals with groups of
persons for spiritual ends.

He deals with them principally in groups: he preaches
to a congregation; he leads the worship of a host; he
is the organizer of groups for purposes of instruction
and service. Just as he ought to know what is taking
place in the minds of people as they worship and work
together, and how the processes serve the aim he has
in mind, so he ought most clearly to know how these
processes are modified, intensified, and changed by the fact
of their being in groups, with many minds and wills
moving at the same time. When he can thus think of a
congregation it becomes not a clinic in which one is im-
passively, coldly conducting certain experiments, nor a collection of isolated individuals, but in itself a force at work.
It is active because it is associated. A congregation is
like an assembling of certain chemicals which, unrelated,
lie apparently inert, but as soon as they are associated
begin to operate in new ways, become a force by association and integration.

A SCHOOL OF SOCIAL LIVING

The great art of life is the art of living together. The fact that we are knowing, feeling, willing, acting persons set in a world of other like persons is the great basic, determinative fact of existence. The adjustment of all these persons, like molecules in the mass that whirl and shift and shape themselves together, is the source of all our morality, all our art, our business, invention, and progress, and, naturally, of all our problems. The actual individual, if ever we could have one, who really lived altogether alone, might have a very simple existence; but it is certain he would neither live very long nor grow very much.

The church, like every other popular institution, deals with us as we live this common social life. It deals with us as we are in our environment, where the personal element, the realities of the many other lives about us, is the most potent force. We are all in this more or less closely fused mass of humanity. We are not the blind, helpless products of the mass. But we cannot escape from it, we cannot shield ourselves from its pressure and impress, and we cannot escape its relations nor the fact and responsibility of our relations to it in all its parts.

THE ENLARGING SOCIETIES

The life of man moves forward in ever enlarging and more complex social groups. His world is first his mother's arms. It enlarges gradually into a universe bounded by the walls of home. This soon pushes itself into the larger world of the neighborhood, playmates and friends and relatives. Some day he steps out into a much larger world:

the school calls him and he becomes a part of the life of the state; it is a world that perhaps appals him by its size; he wonders whether he can ever know all these boys and girls, whether he can learn their games and become familiar with all the unwritten laws of this society.   But he finds his way into that life, and the normal child gradually acquires the habits of social living in the tremendously effective society of the school.   Few fully realize all that this means; in the American public school, real *public* education consists in accustoming the child to live happily, harmoniously, with that strangely mixed social group coming from many kinds of homes, from parentage of many climes, and yet all making up the social unit of the American people.   He is learning there the greatest lesson of his life, the art of living in his large social group.   Later the group may get much larger. By the abilities gained in study he may be able to think the round world into his society, he may have real relations with all men, not only around the present world, but through the ages that have been, and his society may come to include the great of all time.   The church helps him, as the home also should, to see a yet larger society, a fellowship that knows no limits of time or space, that reaches beyond all human persons and makes one a member of the family of God, conscious of a spiritual life that embraces all.   Here is the last and widest of all the circles of man's progressive social experiences, each one necessary and each opening to the willing mind a way into the wider one.

THE SOCIAL LIFE OF THE CHURCH SCHOOL

The church may function in a number of these circles by furnishing necessary experiences and means of development.

For the young it offers small groups of their own kind, in the church-school classes and the like. Such groups are of peculiar efficiency because of their size and flexibility. The class of six or eight has just about the right number of persons for boys or girls. It affords very close social contacts; it permits the working out of the problems of adjustment to other lives in simple forms of experience and under immediate and intimate guidance.

The social-training values of church-school groups have been quite generally neglected or used without serious appreciation of their significance. Undoubtedly, under existing limitations of time, instruction must be the principal activity in such classes, but social adjustments and habituations go on all through the process of instruction and constitute a persistent activity, especially effective because free from consciousness. Socialization continues all the time the group is held together. In many ways it aids the work of instruction; but it does not lessen the need of making it efficient and scientifically sound. To realize and to develop these social potencies is to develop the educational power of the group as a group.

Some teachers are able to see the social values; some owe their success, in spite of lack of training and even in spite of any broad knowledge of subjects taught, to their powers of social organization and direction. But always this work needs supervision. The task is not an easy one. It calls for sympathy, tact, and imagination. Perfunctory direction will not suffice. There is no assurance of anything effectively social in a committee on "social life." That easily degenerates into an agency for promoting artificial cordiality and habitual handshaking. The best forms of social gatherings come normally out of the desires of the groups. What is needed is leaders of vision and insight to set the social processes at work. The minister should know what is taking place wherever lives are grouped. His helpers, the director of religious education and the superintendents of the school, should have an appreciation of social education. Then they will be able to suggest forms of grouping and types of activity which will make the social potencies effective.

These considerations will lead every teacher and director to watch the work of classes, not only with reference to attendance and lesson-learning but also with reference to life-living and especially as to personal relationships. They will bring natural groups together on every possible occasion, under varieties of situations. They will direct them not only to sit together but to play together, to work together, to eat together, and to attempt new enterprises. They will help them to develop group guidance and autonomy through simple organizations, to learn habitually to take certain attitudes toward others and toward other groups by forms of directed association and service.*

SOCIAL LIFE OF YOUNG PEOPLE

The value of social groupings is easily seen when we come to the high-school period and to young manhood and womanhood. But in the churches these groups have not been studied with reference to their essential social possi-

* See, on forms of possible service for children and classes, chap. XIV in *Efficiency in the Sunday School*, Cope (Doran, 1912); *Social Service in the Sunday School* (Univ. of Chicago, 1914), and reports of the Church of the Disciples, Boston.

bilities from the point of view either of instruction or of worship.   Hence we have either "adult classes" in the school or a "young people's" organization conducting so-called devotional meetings and occasionally engaging in forms of church and community service.   That the types of groupings for young people in the church have furnished opportunities for courtship and mating seems to have been regarded as a reproach, as though such inevitable selections would better have been made elsewhere rather than in the church and at other times.   But that reproach rises because we are not accustomed to think sanely of courtship and to regard its higher significances.   We need to see that one of the best things any church could do would be to furnish healthy opportunities for young people to know one another, to know those of the opposite sex in their groups, and to select their mates where the environment would suggest the highest aims and ideals.

All the arguments for coeducation in the college apply to wise provision for the social contacts of young people in the churches.   The fact that they do not avail themselves generally of such opportunities as the churches afford is due not to any inherent, natural depravity on their part but to our fatuous hope that they will adapt themselves to our inflexible institutions and methods, instead of accepting the fact that the institution and method must adapt itself to the life it would aid and lead.   The gregarious instincts of young people stand out and are so commonly recognized that we ought long ago to have made larger provisions for their needs.   It matters not that we may think that young people are simply frivolous and purposeless in following these instincts or that the group of young folks is without serious purposes. In their gatherings they are living out their lives, and they are learning, quite unconsciously, the social life. Perhaps we would prefer to have them less frivolous. But we adults find it hard to understand their ways. Perhaps we wish they would sit around in the sedate circles of our grandmothers' time. But just as we have changed our social ways so must they. We cannot force them to anticipate their later stages. Somewhere these young people will gather and they will be just themselves. Fortunately large numbers of them will be found in homes in couples and in groups just as, probably, they always have been found. But many thousands will be found in other places less innocent and more harmful. The church can hardly reproach them for gathering in dance-halls and at amusement parks so long as she makes no provision for their inevitable gregariousness and affords no opportunity for the free exercise of their social instincts.

SOCIAL ENDEAVORS

There has been a marked tendency to neglect those gatherings which were called simply social. This tendency has developed partly as a result of the belief that they lay outside the spiritual function of the church and still more because the social instincts of the young have been capitalized by agents of commercial amusement. There was a profound reason for calling these informal and often apparently purposeless gatherings "socials," for they were really the exercises of the young in the social life; they were the endeavors of those who were newly entered consciously on social living to adjust themselves and learn its art.

The young people's society was one of the outstanding

forms of this type of social grouping. It succeeded in the degree that it met the natural spiritual social needs of young people; it failed as it was diverted to other and factitious ends. The history of these societies shows how irrepressible are the social instincts of youth. In the face of opposition, in spite of exploitation and regardless of many instances of decline and failure they persist in one form or another. We ought to take time to consider this type of organization in the light of the essential nature and needs of those in the group.*

Greater wisdom is now being used in the direction of the energies of young people. We recognize the passion of the young for activity and, along with this, their strong tendency toward idealization. They are the people who under normal conditions believe in a better world, a finer society, in the possibility of realizing life's ideals, and who have the energy to attempt to make real their ideals. Wise direction of these groups into fields of ideal community service is bound to be educationally helpful. In service they give expression to their ideals and they learn to take life in terms of helpful work. By experience they learn the conditions and means of service and in the course of such work they also learn to live and work together. They engage in surveys of communities, in direct relief of distress, in ministries to the sorrowing, the needy, the shut-ins, prisoners, and the sick. They engage in civic-betterment work, in promoting plans for community improvement, and in civic and political work.

The dangers are that this work shall become consciously

* See chapter on "Young People," where the special needs of this group are discussed.

that of "uplift," work in which the worker assumes an attitude of superiority, or that it shall be a result of mere zeal for reforming in order to make others do the things we would like to have them do. It may be only the purposeless ambition to stir up something, to make at least a fuss, and to carry on a campaign of mere criticism and often vilification. Most of these dangers are inherent, however, in any kind of associated effort for community and civic betterment.

One danger especially confronts the success and maintenance of this form of social activity for young people, and that is that it shall lose its essential social qualities and fail to furnish opportunities for developing the group feeling and spirit. Reformers are prone each to sally forth on his own mission and to become sterile products of zeal without human feeling and social moderation. The young need to spend much of their time in their own group. Such time can be wisely used in reporting on their experiences and in general conference on their plans. The same young people who with spontaneous enthusiasm spend hours discussing plans for what we call a "social function" will show the same joy and zeal, the same animation in discussing plans for useful, altruistic social work.

Attention is directed to activities because they are the clue to social organization. Definite projects of usefulness are like magnetic poles inviting like-minded persons. The project fuses the group into social unity. As it is carried forward it enriches the social life. The pleasures of co-operation and of many common experiences create strong spiritual ties. Working together is the best way of learning to live together. The project which thus unites a group owes much of its social effectiveness to the fact that the social process is an unconscious one.

The project as the means of organizing and developing the social life is fully as effective with children. A common purpose which is to them evidently real and worth while calls out their co-operative powers.* It reveals the ways of social living and it furnishes the emotional experiences of the social life. Activity of a purposeful character for the group is the secret of social organization. This is a recognized principle in the modern school, where activity is stimulated and directed by the "project," that is, the purpose or aim which enlists and organizes activities.

REFERENCES

ADDAMS, JANE, *The Spirit of Youth and the City Streets* (Macmillan, 1909).

KING, IRVING, *Social Aspects of Education* (Macmillan, 1912).

SWIFT, EDGAR J., *Youth and the Race* (Scribners, 1912).

* See "New Forms of Class Teaching," by Lavinia Tallmann, in *Religious Education* for August, 1917.

CHAPTER XII

SOCIAL SERVICE IN THE EDUCATIONAL PROGRAMME

PRACTICALLY, it is still an open question whether the church should engage in social service. Theoretically, there are only a few small groups doubting, but, so far as action is concerned, the majority everywhere hesitates. Few have any real programmes of service in their communities; a great many satisfy themselves with occasional expositions of social duty or an exciting exposé of some civic ill. Except for sporadic ministries of relief, the tendency is to substitute discussion and definition of these duties for doing them.

THE MOTIVE

The motive for social service is native to the Christian character; whoever has the mind of Christ cannot refrain either the loving hand of aid or the earnest effort to realize the Christian ideal of society. If the individual Christian normally is thus socially moved, is it conceivable that Christians socialized in a church group can be less influenced by such motives, can be less social when socialized? If social love is an individual duty it must be none the less a duty for the society. This motive of love is the only one that can direct the church in social action. The ecclesiastical record of "social service" would be quite different if the motive of love had been the only one operative. Certainly there have

132

been instances where the motives have been those of falling into a popular vogue, winning a reputation for striking activity, or offering a bait to the multitude. Wherever the church has calculated her profits in the enterprise she has made a poor investment and brought an ill savor on her work.

When Josiah Strong wrote *The New Era** we were sure that the day of the institutional church had come. Why has it been so slow in dawning? Why, except for a few outstanding exceptions, has the institutional church failed? Is it not at least in part because we hailed the idea of the institutional church, not so much as a means of saving society, but rather as a means of saving the church? The institutional type of service seemed to be a good thing to promote in the degree that it would win friends and fame to the church. Social service was a good advertising feature. But "features," as such, have always failed, and we might as well let social service alone until we can see that it has a real place, an essential part, in the inevitable programme of the church.

SOCIAL SERVICE AND EDUCATION

Some have thought that the educational programme was a reaction from the tendency to emphasize social service. Perhaps this has been true in separate instances. Occasionally a church has swung from the feverish bustle of institutional activity to seek refuge in the calm repose of lectures and classes. But this simply indicates that as they knew not social service so they do not know education. The two are not opposed; they are inseparable. No church has an educational programme unless it is fully committed

* Baker & Taylor, 1903.

to doing the will of God in society and to leading others to do that will.

SOCIAL SERVICE AND RELIGION

The essential place of social service in the educational programme of the church lies—

First : In *the social nature* of the work or process of *religious education.* In fact, it lies in the basic social nature of all education. This becomes vividly apparent when education is seen, not as classes and instruction, but as a process of developing lives, the lives of social persons under social conditions and for social ends. The aim of religious education in the church is the development of persons, as religious beings, in a social group, toward a religious ideal of character—an ideal essentially one of social love and helpfulness—and toward a whole society realizing the ideal of a brotherhood of persons in this world.

Second : Considering in detail the aim—to develop persons as religious beings—the place of social service lies in *the nature of religion.* We cannot think of persons developing except in their social relations; they are persons because they live with other persons. They grow in personality as there are developed the powers of knowing others, adjusting life to others, serving others, and thus discovering the values of the spiritual social order. Religion is for the children of to-day a social concept; it means seeing life in its relations to other lives and to the great Life of all. One cannot think of a Christian individual in terms of pure individualism. True, much popular theology* goes as far as any thinking can go in individualism; it appeals to the

* See John H. Holmes, in *Religion for Today,* 1917.

crassest individual motives; it describes the terms of salvation as a contract between individuals, one a God and the other a man, irrespective of all the rest of the personal universe. Yet, so basic is the social consciousness that even the individualistic theologian only postpones his social ideals to another world. Somewhere the religious spirit is compelled to find its social realization; even though contractual salvation offers a pass "good only for the bearer," it is, nevertheless, a pass to Zion, the far-off social Utopia. The ideals of that remote heavenly social order are often primitive and its details vague; but evidently even where the social interest is most urgently denied the social nature of religion will not be denied its rights. It is impossible to educate a religious being save as a social being.

Third: Not only does the social ideal dominate all modern religious thinking, but social processes are also *the only possible processes* adapted to the ends of religious education. It may be possible for one alone, buried with books or lost in research, to gain much knowledge, but, for the purposes of education, he must come out of such isolation and learn life amongst lives.

A worthy ideal of social service in the church will lead to the development of every possible opportunity for lives to be lived together, in the social whole. Somehow we must get away from the petty, mechanical notions of social service as the organization of basket-laden, slum-bent delegations. The church needs to understand that for which the settlement primarily stands, that folks want folks; they need men more than ministrations. The best ministry of all is that of living amongst those who need us. We would talk a good deal less about social service if we could break down the unchristian caste lines in our religious practices, for, really living together, such service would be as simple, as non-phenomenal, as the old-time custom of exchanging doughnuts and cookies across the back fence. We are never conscious of doing social service to our neighbors, but then we are doing it best and most.

SOCIAL HABITUATIONS

Frequently we fail to develop Christians because we are not offering people a real Christian environment. This spiritual life develops as, living with all others, one forgets caste, ignores conventional barriers of wage and salary, and, by sharing life, discovers the permanent and real values of personality common to all kinds of people who really love the good and the eternal. The church is often so influenced by social custom that there is very little social mingling. Just as in the city the different communions divide into rich churches, or rather churches for the rich (quite a different thing) and churches for the poor, so in the village the sectarian lines frequently represent actual social cleavages. The result is that boys and girls grow up in religious institutions that emphasize caste lines, that are much less democratic, socially much less Christian, than the public high school. In religious living they associate only with those of their own social grade. If they are at all affluent they may "go in for social service" and become acquainted with the poor at the end of a charity basket.

A RELIGIOUS SOCIETY

Perhaps the man with money needs the poor man more than the poor man needs the rich; but the essential fact is that we all need one another; none of us can live either to himself or to his class. The real programme of the church must make us think more of a Christian society, and that will mean less need for what we call Christian social service. We all need to know one another; we need to really live as members of one family—or cease the family prayer. That does not mean living under one roof, though it ought to mean worshipping under one. It does not mean that all the circumstances of life will always be alike for all; but it does mean that we shall think deeper than things, that we shall act upon the common spiritual life we have and enter into the real society of persons, of spirits in which no man is rich or poor by the measure of goods but only by the Godlike graces of life. We can never have a religious world until we do this; we can never carry forward the real educational programme of the church in leading men into Godlikeness and this world into the place of his will until we can live together at least as a common religious society.

This closer, kindlier social living is needed by growing young people to save them from the habits of social cleavage. It is needed by those who have much goods to save them from hardness of heart, from forgetting that a man's life does not consist in the abundance of things he possesses, from the complacency that in time makes unreal the sufferings and handicaps of those who have not. It is needed by the poor in goods that they may really have the fulness of their spiritual rights of brotherhood, that they may give to others their virtues of fortitude and patience, that they may help all to know from the inside of experience what the real problems of society are. It is needed to save us all from "benevolence" with its attendant diseases of parasitism and

social astigmatism.   It is needed to save us from the fast-
developing social habit of subsidizing social enterprises with
largess, predicating social enterprises on the generosity, the
whim, even the hoodwinking of those who have the world's
money.

A PRACTICABLE IDEAL SOCIETY

The personal Christian character can grow only in a
Christian society.   We cannot yet organize all society on
the Christian ideal, though it seems to be coming; but we
can have in the church a society which, at least in many
respects, is, in actual life, such a society.   Life in it, when it
is really a society of the spiritual life, animated and guided
by the divine ideals, will bring all its members under the
most efficient means of Christian education.   At the same
time such a society teaches the world what religion means
and what Christianity means.

The church itself then serves in social education as a social
institution.   It is the "ecclesia," the gathering of persons.
Wherever they gather about a common spiritual ideal there
is a church.   The one essential ordinance is this gathering,
this communion of persons, of souls.   But wherever persons
are associated social processes are at work and in a sense
education is operative.   The largest educational activity
of a church is just this socialization of persons.   We cannot too strongly emphasize this.   A class functions more
in being a class than in its course of study.   A school
educates more through the organized experience of its
"crowd" than through its curriculum of studies.   "Forsake
not the assembling of yourselves," not because of any
dictum of authority, nor alone even because of what we

may do at the assembly, but because of what the assembling does for us.

The Christian ideal of personal character is a social ideal; the aim of the church is to develop a society of Christlike socially minded persons. That ideal reaches out into a complete social concept of religion. The church seeks socially minded persons organized into a religious society. In fact, the realization of the ideal for the person is largely dependent on the realization of the ideal for the society, as the latter determines the former. Persons grow according to their social, personal environment. The mass determines the molecule. The church does not seek to grow in spiritual beauty heavenly plants perfected in some celestial atmosphere, but it realizes that it is dealing with human beings set down in the soil of every-day life. The interest of the church, therefore, is in the soil in which souls grow, as the interest of the educator is in the determination of environment.*

SAVING SOCIETY

But we must reach out beyond the church. Socially it is a means and not an end. We must dominate society in order to provide a soil for the soul. We must save the world or the world will prevent salvation. So long as we think of religion as an other-worldly, ethereal affair dealing with unrelated things called souls we can question the social imperative. But organized religion is influencing directly persons who feel and think and act; it is developing them, in powers of feeling and thought and action, into a real spiritual society. The church must face and solve the problems

* See Chapter XIII, " The Church and Community Welfare."

of society, not because it is the spectacular thing to do so, but because social conditions are tremendously potent in the same field. They are determining the characters of men and the character of society. They have a vital and essential share in the immediate function of the church in the world. She cannot make lives anew in a world that remains essentially unchanged.

The church, moreover, is forbidden to slight her social duty by the unvarying law that neither the person nor the group can grow except by service. As a teacher the church makes no permanent impression on persons until her teaching is expressed in action. Service is one of the normal methods of translating doctrine into deed, of doing the will. Nothing is ours in the world of ideals until we carry it over into the world of action. Social service in the church is religious education carrying instruction and inspiration forward into action. The church is much more than an institution in which pious persons cultivate their abilities to absorb spiritual instruction. Those who have done no more than listen to sermons have died spiritually of homiletical dyspepsia. They have worn out the pews when they ought to have been wearing out the pavements. They have listened when they ought to have lifted. But together modern education and modern religion have been insisting, with increasing harmony, on action. If the church is to educate men into religious character she must constantly furnish opportunities to put into action all that is taught. Make real the ideal or it fades. This is a fundamental educational principle.

Evidently social service is more significant than an ephemeral interest or a special department of church work. It is a concrete expression of the attitude of the church toward life, and it is a mode of carrying forward the educational task of the church. It may well be doubted whether, under such an ideal, social service can be treated as a separate department in the organization of a church, just as hygiene would not be a separate department in a well-regulated family or institution. It will be seen rather as a controlling principle which at present needs practical interpretation.

PRACTICAL APPLICATIONS

Something has already been done in the direction of applying the principle of service in the educational work of the church with children.* For example, in the church-school service activities have been studied with reference to the opportunities which they afford to the different grades of the school. At the same time these activities have been related to the teaching material so that the child is able to carry over into action that which he has received in the form of instruction.† The arrangement of a curriculum of activity is a task of great difficulty. It can easily become purely mechanical and therefore meaningless. It must be flexible, determined by local conditions and the lives of those who participate. Some forms of service are common to almost all churches and all communities.‡ But in every case the value of programmes will be greatly increased when they

---

* See *Graded Social Service in the Sunday School*, by W. H. Hutchins (University of Chicago Press, 1914).

† A good example is *A Course for Beginners in Religious Education*, by M. E. Rankin (Scribners, 1917), in which service is made the foundation of all the lessons.

‡ Besides the much more comprehensive survey by Dr. Hutchins, the author ventured, in *Efficiency in the Sunday School* (1912), to give a list of activities for boys which was based on experience in a small church. There are a number of good examples in *Graded Missionary Education in the Church School*, by Frederica Beard (A.B.P.S., 1917).

are carefully worked out and frequently revised for each school in the light of its own needs. In doing this certain principles must be followed. They are the principles which are applied by asking the questions concerning a programme of activities: What needs to be done? What persons or groups are best suited to these tasks?—that is, not principally who are best fitted by experience, but who are best suited in view of their needs and their characteristics? What is the relation of the activities proposed to any others preceding and succeeding? What instruction should precede the service contemplated? What should follow?

Underlying all the organization of specific programmes there must be definite plans for general training in the social aspects of the religious life. It is important to see how real and definite and inclusive are the social-service aspects of the educational programme. It includes all that goes to make real the ideal of a religious society, a God-willed world. It includes whatever men do to make the community the kind of a place in which the will of God can be done. It sees the possibilities of the community as a force to do the will of God. This does not mean regulating the lives of our fellows so that they will do just what we have determined God wants them to do. It means organizing a community so that by its health, its powers for happiness, for growth, and for righteousness it works as a force to make happy, right willing and right living people. It regards all the services of the church as forces to realize the religious society. It includes all that makes homes better, more capable for their work, streets safer, playgrounds and parks more helpful to lives, factories more efficient to serve society. It thinks of factories making men as well as dividends. It reaches out into all the world to realize the good of man through the means of the social organizations.

When one sees the social vision in its fulness our schemes and our details of method may appear petty and insignificant. But plans we must have. This is more than a glowing dream; it is a realizable ideal. It comes only through actions that seem small in the light of the whole. The first step will be the education of the church in the social meanings of religion. Somehow men must be quickened to see that this real, practical life of daily experience and living together is that which is making us all, and this is the sphere where religion must be realized. This is not a "social gospel"; it is a life fact. The good news is not that society saves men; it is that God wills their eternal good, their salvation in terms of infinite love, that he wills it all for the salvation of the whole. And the working fact is that those who are to be saved are living in society, growing in it as plants in a soil, and they cannot be saved in any full sense except as the whole is lifted together. "God so loved the world." What are we doing for the world? And what are we letting the world do with men? The vision of the people must be clarified. Such simple standards as those defined in *The Social Creed of the Churches* show how fundamental they are to any religious concept of social conditions.*

SOCIAL STUDIES

Young people must be trained in the habits of the Christian social life. Their grouping in the normal society of the

* See Reports of the Commission on Christian Service in the Federal Council of Churches of Christ in America, and such a book as *A Social Theory of Religious Education*, George A. Coe, shows how fundamental are the social facts in education.

Christian brotherhood will be the most important step in that training. They must take up the simple daily duties of a religious social order. They will begin in their every-day relations, in the family, on the playground, in the public schools, or wherever they are.* We must cease to teach social duties as occasional and extraneous to their lives. Those who carry baskets in benevolence must habitually carry themselves as religious persons to all other persons. Social self-giving will express itself in all social experiences, on the street, playground, or school floor. The social life will be learned by living it. All special teachings, discussions, definitions will come later; they will rise out of actual experience. Lessons are learned as they are lived. Our social courses for young people will develop as we take them out into the practice fields of life.†

But the teaching cannot be neglected. The immediate duty would seem to be that we shall revise much of it in the light of social living. This laboratory of daily living where youth is practising the religious social order may dictate our lessons. Too many of the courses of study are purely academic discussions of Old World persons, Old World acts, and Old World theories. How unreal they are! Is there any wonder they do not issue in life when the learner thinks of them only as tasks? They are something to be done, he knows not why, and he is burning with impatience to get into the real world, living, actual, thrilling, just beyond the

* As a text see *Christianizing the Community*, by Harry F. Ward, Association Press, 1917.

† See *The Social Welfare Work of Unitarian Churches*, E. S. Forbes, pamphlet free (American Unitarian Association), and *Wise Direction of Church Activities Towards Social Welfare*, Chas. W. Eliot, free pamphlet (American Unitarian Association).

classroom walls. Suppose we were to do more as Jesus did, take our lessons from the immediate life? Would they be real? Could they be lived? Would they not be most truly religious if they interpreted the things the boy knows, the baseball game, the civic struggle, the city council in terms of God's plan for a world? Which does this boy need most, to know why and when and how Israel marched seven times around Jericho or how his playground may be a place where right and truth and godliness prevail? Does he not need to know how he shall live just now and what the life of all about him should be? If we cannot make spiritual the immediate then our spirituality is only a dream of the past. And to this immediate we may bring the heritage of the rich past. Then history has meaning as it brings light for to-day. The wealth of tradition, heroism, and idealism in the long race story are essential to strengthen and inspire the life of the present. But they, too, are real only as they are realized in the life of to-day.

Social service, then, is an essential part of the educational programme of the church because it is the means by which the ideal of a Christian society is to be realized and, at the same time, it affords the means by which the religious life and character is developed. What could afford us greater encouragement than the fact that churches are fast coming to see this duty and opportunity? In the modern church the youth who have seen their visions may also invest their energies in making the visions real. In these churches each life is finding itself in losing itself, is gaining fulness of life in self-giving.

REFERENCES

Coe, George A., *A Social Theory of Religious Education* (Scribners, 1917).

Holmes, John Haynes, *The Revolutionary Function of the Modern Church* (Putnams, 1912).

Macfarland, C. S., *Christian Service and the Modern World* (Revell, 1915).

Cutting, R. F., *Church and Society* (Macmillan, 1912).

Taylor, Graham, *Religion and Social Action* (Dodd, Mead, 1913).

Ward, H. F., *The Social Creed of the Churches* (Abingdon, 1914).

Trawick, A. M., *The City Church and Its Social Mission* (Association Press, 1913).

Batten, S. Z., *The Social Task of Christianity* (Revell, 1911).

The Federal Council of Churches *Year Book* contains a list of the pamphlets issued by the various church boards and commissions on social service.

Vol. II, Men and Religion Reports, *Social Service* (Association Press, 1912).

CHAPTER XIII

THE CHURCH AND COMMUNITY WELFARE

THE concern of the church in community welfare is based on the social character of the church and the social nature of education. The community is the social environment of the church; it constitutes the life soil in which her people are growing. The responsibility of the church for conditions of living has been suggested in the chapter on "Social Service," but there are relations of the church to the life of the community which demand special attention. The community offers an educational problem to the church in two aspects: First, as a prophetic teaching institution the church must educate the community in the ideals and habits of civic, social righteousness. Second, the community is in itself an educational power, very largely determining the lives for which the church is responsible.

It may be profitable to study the two simple types of communities existing to-day, what is called generally the rural type—that is, where the problems of intense human polarization do not exist—and the city type. The first field illustrates the essential principles that prevail in all community living. The neglected needs of rural life and the fact that here there is a larger freedom of opportunity give this special problem first place. Further, whatever may be true in the city, community organization is the largest opportunity of the church in the country.

THE RURAL COMMUNITY

The country church, made familiar to us by some of the best in English literature, was so human an institution because it was so intensely interested in the welfare of the persons in its community. The American village church always has been a ministering institution. A large measure of its activities have been directed informally to the care of the sick, provision for the needy, and relief of the distressed. Goldsmith's parson, "passing rich on forty pounds a year," never turning a beggar from the door; Trollope's parson's wife, who spends her days in piecing out flannel petticoats for villagers; Margaret Deland's charming charities in Old Chester; and the ladies' aid society of the American church, with its quiltings and its buzzing sewing-machines, all rise from the same great dynamic of human regard for the welfare of others. They are united in love though divided in time and creeds.

But in these days the aid society has almost passed out of existence; the parson's wife no longer wins awesome obeisance as the potential petticoat distributer and the church is by no means the sole agency for the relief of distress. They are no longer the dominant factors in the determination of community welfare. Welfare work is organized; it has become a science and it demands more than a programme of amateur beneficence.

The churches have not been blind to the social changes of the past decades. They are adapting themselves to the new community life, but their adaptations, as yet, are largely in the experimental stage. They lack fundamental guiding principles. Much is being done, but a large part of the activity is simply a response to the conviction that "something must be done about it." Many churches in the larger villages and cities have fairly adequate programmes. They have determined their relations to the social agencies of the community. They are co-operating with them, and their field is clearly marked out by the recognition of their special responsibility for persons as religious beings and for conditions that make for a religious society.

In the cities, boards of charity, relief, and philanthropy, together with purely civic organizations, carry on organized social work. But in the rural districts there is scarcely any organized provision for community welfare, for the church, the social unit of the country, is only beginning to realize a responsibility for social well-being. Rural churches have been losing their former social contacts largely because their communities have been undergoing social disintegration.*

RURAL CONDITIONS

The most striking problem of rural life at this time is its lack of social unity. Present conditions are due to a number of causes: immigration to the country has broken up racial integrity; many a community has people of half a dozen nationalities owning or renting its farms; none of them has been in the melting-pot long enough to become fused; the increasing social compactness of the city intensifies the feeling of separateness in the country; the proximity of growing villages has broken links of rural unity, such as neighborly exchange, service, and opportunities for acquaintance at store and post-office. The trolley has often disin-

* See Warren H. Wilson on "The Function of the Church in the Country," in *Religious Education* for Feb., 1918.

tegrated a community by taking away mutual dependencies. The country lags behind the city in its thinking on social affairs; it is still individualistic. If diphtheria breaks out on Smith's farm, the neighbors think, not of contagion in the community, but of aches and pains and distresses in the Smith household. The country church, very much like the city church, lags so far behind the human procession in its thinking on social matters that it has no message on social subjects. They are often tabooed as unspiritual, as too worldly. Much accessible material on social conditions is so exclusively urban that the minister finds it difficult to deal with the rural problem.*

Yet even in the country the church can no more escape community responsibility than it can escape the simple fact of its community environment. This is so, primarily, because every church is a community organization. Regardless of ecclesiastical theories, the fact remains that every church is the communal grouping of kindred spirits seeking common aims, bound by common ideals and sympathies. The spirit of this age which thinks of welfare, not in terms of individualism but in terms of society, has begun to penetrate the church. It is being accepted by its leaders, and soon the churches will throw their united social force into the realization of social ideals. The country church will come to realize its community responsibility, to see that it has a primary task of securing right physical and moral conditions in the rural districts, and that it has a deeper concern in hygiene, sanitation, and recreation than it has in platting prospective subdivisions in another world.

* See Henry Israel, *County Church and Community Cooperation* (Association Press).

When a church turns her attention to clean streets, to healthy homes, to recreation centres, to means of social accretion and integration, she is not forsaking her divine mission; she is cultivating heavenly character by appropriate means.

THE POSSIBILITIES

What can a rural church do for community welfare? Such a church can come to an intelligent understanding of community conditions, needs, and possibilities. A chart of a rural community, showing the homes, churches, schools, places of communal gathering, locations of agencies for good and for ill, would prove as striking as such charts have been for city wards. The church may set its young men to gather the facts and prepare such a chart.*

The rural church often already has the plant with which to begin social-centre operations. The great need is better social fusing. The lines of racial differences and the preoccupations of intensified business have put an end to social visiting. We do not know one another. The church service should be strengthened at the point of opportunity for social acquaintance. The church building can be used for such attractions as will bring the community together for recreation and for self-improvement. A rural community needs band concerts, lectures, concerts, a library, and suitable recreation just as truly as a city community. Why should not the local church undertake these things? They have been carried on successfully in many instances. They

* On the method of the survey, see *Knowing One's Own Community*, by Carol Aronovici, a very valuable free pamphlet published by the American Unitarian Association, Boston. Also, *Community Surveys*, by C. S. Carrol (Abingdon Press, 1915).

afford an opportunity not only for the church to minister but for all people to find opportunities for service and for each to find his own ministry to all. Many a youth who would otherwise drift, through idleness, into vice will find himself at his best when he has a chance to work at a playground or at the library activities in the church.

We can easily revive certain now obsolete activities for the rural church, obsolete only because they failed to make necessary readjustments. They are: philanthropic service, once accomplished by the parson, now to be accomplished by systematic, directed study of community needs by groups of capable persons; library work, once conducted by the Sunday-school library, now by co-operation with library centres for the distribution of all good literature through the week; the reading-room, once attempted as a bait to church affiliation, now to become the social centre for the community, the place where men worship God by getting to know one another better; the playing-ground, once found in many churchyards, the place where the old sat under the trees, looked over the graves of the dead and gossiped about the living, while the children played on the green, now easily possible to many a country church with its adjacent acres of field and farm. Why should not the ball-ground be next the church? The problem of Sunday ball-playing would then solve itself. The church has lost control—moral control—of many things because she has heedlessly and often selfishly divorced herself from them.

CO-OPERATION

Where there are several rural churches co-operation becomes imperative. The present duplications of plant and organization are scandalously wasteful. In the economy.

of righteousness religion must give an account for its wastes. If half the rural churches could be abolished and one-fourth could be relocated the situation would be vastly improved. But, looking forward, it is possible to prevent waste and inefficiency by avoiding the creation of unnecessary welfare organizations. To have as many gymnasiums or playing-grounds as there are churches is, in the country, a terrible exhibition of the blindness of bigotry. The situation demands the syndication of energies and organizations.

If the church is to serve the community its work can be done only on the basis of unselfish service and only through community co-operation. The most common difficulty is that as soon as the A church attempts a programme of community service the B church duplicates it lest the A's should seem to get any advantage over them. Only as all syndicate their efforts, avoid the dreadful wastes of duplication and competition, and present to the community plans of united service can we hope really to accomplish the organization of the community as the environment of the higher life, the soil of the soul. The Y. M. C. A. forms an efficient and ready agency through which the local churches may carry on their physical welfare work and their social service for young men. Given the support of the churches, the Young Women's Christian Association affords a like agency for girls and young women. In all endeavors all the churches must get together to discover the best means of effecting their common ends.

PREPARATION

The programme of the church must be more effective in inspiring and educating men to do things for the community. She must establish the ideal of a community life favorable to the development of aggressive, competent, righteous character, and she must teach, train, and inspire her people to the making of such a community. The mission and opportunity of preaching in shaping ideals and determining action is clear; the question is whether the preacher is quite clear as to community ideals and their importance. On this waits any specific, organized instruction of the people through classes and courses of study. We need courses of study in home-making, parenthood, domestic welfare, and all that concerns the institution in which character is most determined. We need courses in civics and in social religion. We need studies of community experiences and service to acquaint people with progress in other places. We need, in a word, all that will teach character development through the machinery and forces of the community.* The church school is one great opportunity for this work. There ought to come a time in the life of youth when the literary study of the Bible receives practical application in this direction, when he will fix his eyes on the place and conditions in which he and others must now work out heroism and sane sanctity. The fact is, he is already far more interested in his real and immediate life than in any discussions of historical or literary views and he wants only direction to apply himself to work.

But the church school may be advantageously supplemented by other groups meeting on week evenings. Clubs

---

* Something has been done to prepare text-books: *The Gospel of the Kingdom* (American Institute of Social Service); Kent, *Social Teachings of the Prophets and Jesus;* Weston, *The World a Field of Christian Service;* Jenks and Kent, *Making of a Nation* and *Testing of a Nation's Ideals;* Ward and Edwards, *Christianizing Community Life;* Forbush, *Child Study and Child Training.*

and like organizations from all the churches may together follow well-arranged programmes of study provided they are sufficiently elementary, evidently practical, and led by persons willing to learn. Such courses are already prepared;* churches are using them, and the chances are that before long the country dweller will understand his life and deal with it more scientifically than will any other. He will deal with it effectively when he takes it as a means and opportunity for the development of fulness of personality and competency of character.

THE CITY CHURCH

The special problems of the urban church,† though by no means entirely peculiar to them, are those due to the crowded programme of city life. Many of them have been evident in the rural situation. They rise in the more highly developed socialization of life, so that the interests of persons pass over from the smaller groups, as families and churches, into the larger groups for amusement and recreation. Play has passed from the back-yard into the park, entertainment from the family group around the piano to the amusement park and the moving-picture show. The situation is fraught with danger because guiding controls

---

* *Civic Righteousness and Civic Pride*, N. M. Hall (Sherman, French, 1914). *Social Work*, English, W. E. Chadwick (Longmans, 1909). *The Social Gospel*, Shailer Mathews (Griffith & Rowland, 1910). International Graded, Senior, Fourth Year, *The Bible and Social Religion*. *Social Duties from the Christian Point of View*, C. R. Henderson (Univ. of Chicago Press, 1909). *Society, Its Origin and Development*, H. K. Rowe (Scribners).

† On the general programme of community usefulness, see the chapter on "Social Service." See also *The Socialized Church*, by Worth M. Tippy (Eaton & Mains, 1909).

are removed and the motives of commercial exploitation are substituted for those of informal friendly pleasure. The situation is so familiar that it needs no amplification.

THE AMUSEMENT PROBLEM

We face a newly awakened recognition of the necessity of recreation. People are believing in play; the pressure of life forces us all to seek relief. The opportunities in recreation and amusement are recognized by those who capitalize them for revenue, and we have failed to develop in ourselves the powers of self-entertainment. All this is accentuated by the current tendency to take all life in terms of pleasure alone.

What is a reasonable programme for a church facing the present passion for amusement and seeking to minister to the normal needs of humanity in this respect? The church must protect the rights of the people. First, the right to play,* to means of recreation, restraining those who would turn innocent pleasures into debauching excesses solely for purposes of gain. Second, the social right to moral health. No one has a right to spread either physical infection or moral infection. We who quarantine contagious diseases have a clear right to quarantine the carriers and exploiters of moral perversions and ills. No pleas of the rights of money, vested interests, or business can take precedence of the rights of men and women to morally healthful conditions.

What, practically, can the local church do in the present situation? Its minister may simply denounce the present-

* See *The Church and the People's Play*, by H. A. Atkinson (Pilgrim Press, 1915). *The Church and the Young Man's Game*, F. J. Milnes, (Doran, 1913).

day "craze for amusements"; he may roundly condemn dancing and the opera.* Much pulpit condemnation of amusements exhibits powers of imagination rather than observation. Denunciation will not be enough. Whatever is done we cannot escape the fact that growing natures must have some means of meeting the needs which at present they seek to satisfy through amusements. They must have free, associated, voluntary, and ideal activities. Young people are like children in the growing period; their rapid development makes play as much a necessity as food. With them play takes the form of recreations, social gatherings, the dance, attendance on theatres, movies, and the parks. These things, in some degree at least, offer some satisfaction to the craving for ideal experiences. No matter what our tastes may be, we cannot hope to have a community free from play, one in which every person over fifteen spends all his leisure reading serious books. Nor can we expect that young people will ever be old people. In fact, we are recognizing the benefits of play so generally that to-day we have no old people.

Nor can the church neglect this play life. The young person is growing in character, good or bad, in the hours of play. This personal life is usually being determined more by the leisure hours than by any others. The religious life is being determined; this life does not grow by being dipped into the devotional developer of a church service once a week; it grows all the time. If the church seeks the development of religious persons she has a deep concern in all that makes for or hinders their growth anywhere or at any

* On these amusements, see chap. V in *The Church and the People's Play*, Atkinson; *Popular Amusements*, R. H. Edwards (Association Press, 1915).

time. We would not ban amusements if we could; we cannot ignore them; we have but one thing to do, *to determine what they shall be.*

RECREATION SURVEY

The first step will be to know the facts of this part of the community's life.* With the aid of workers in the church or in co-operation with a general community agency we must gather the facts of the life of amusement and recreation. Get all the facts and tabulate them. Then exhibit the facts in graphic form by means of maps and charts. Show this exhibit publicly. The survey furnishes the facts to guide the church in strengthening the helpful agencies, developing healthful opportunities and exposing and eliminating all that injures. Now is the time to determine what the community needs and to plan to supply sound, helpful, attractive recreation and amusement.† If possible, all such provision should be made in co-operation with every other church and with such agencies as the public school, the library, the Y. M. and Y. W. C. A. In one community the local church furnished so good a grade of motion-pictures that the village council voted to exclude all commercialized "movies" and to leave this form of amusement to that church.‡

COMMUNITY ORGANIZATION

A pressing problem of the community lies in the lack of organization for life's higher purposes. The ideal agencies are in bitter competition at some points while at others

* On the survey of recreation, see part III of *Popular Amusements*, by R. H. Edwards (Association Press, 1915).

† See *Community Music and Drama*, a valuable pamphlet published by the Extension Division, Univ. of Wisconsin, 1917; 10 cents.

‡ Winnetka, Ill., under direction of Rev. J. W. F. Davies.

they wholly neglect their opportunities. There is often a sense of conflict between the school and the churches, sometimes between the churches and the Christian associations. There is no common consciousness of a united community programme in which each agency plays a suitable part. If we could have a real programme we might begin to think of our communities in educational terms. We might see that in a very real sense this larger common life is an effective school in which all are learning to live. We might unite to make it really a school of religious living.

The immediate need in every community is for an organization through which the churches and other agencies seeking ideal ends might co-operate. We need that which corresponds to the city council, a group representing every cause and activity for good, bringing them together and expressing their will. Something could be provided in the nature of a Community Council of Religious Education in which each church and each church school, each public school, library, and like organization or institution would have membership. Through their representatives the churches and the other agencies would co-operate to study the field, to plan co-ordinated provision for all the needs of youth, to co-operate in all their own plans, to avoid duplication and competition, and to prepare, advertise, and execute a unified programme for the entire community. That would avoid the present conflicts and difficulties due to independent and unstudied action.*

* Keep in touch with all wider community organizations. State-wide movements are being formed. A good example is the "A Better Community Movement of Illinois," Robert E. Hieronymus, University, Ill., Community Adviser. The convention of the Religious Education Association in 1918 was devoted to "organizing the community."

Attention has been paid to recreation in this chapter, not because it is thought to be the only problem, but because it is so pertinent and so well illustrates the method in the many fields suggested in the chapter on "Social Service."

The most important relation of the church to community welfare will be an educational one. Our interest and activity in doing things must never be allowed to eclipse the duty of the church as an inspirational agency. It may be a good thing to organize the men of the church into a road-scraping brigade, but it is better by far to carry out a programme of so systematically inspiring those men with the ideals of the rightly adjusted community that they will never be contented with anything less than the realization of the ideal. The direct service of a church in community welfare justifies itself only as an essential part of the educational programme of that church. Primarily and ultimately, the ideal community depends upon ideal character, and ideal character comes about through inspiration, leadership, nurture, and service under conditions that foster personal growth. In all our thinking about community welfare we must often look beyond mechanisms to the product and beyond the physical conditions which determine life to life itself. Nor must we make the fatal error of confounding means with end, of urging people to live merely for clean streets, libraries, playgrounds, and æsthetic pleasures. The church must take her place of leadership in developing all these agencies to their highest efficiency and in applying them with the greatest economy to the product of the better, saner, and finer life.

REFERENCES

I. GENERAL

STRAYER, P. M., *Reconstruction of the Church*, part II, chap. IV (Macmillan, 1915).

EARP, EDWIN L., *Social Aspects of Religious Institutions* (Eaton & Mains, 1908).

CARROLL, C. E., *Community Survey* (Abingdon Press, 1915).

ARONOVICI, CAROL, *Knowing One's Own Community* (American Unitarian Association; free).

EDWARDS, R. H., *Popular Amusements*, part III, on "Survey of Recreation" (Association Press, 1915).

WARD, HARRY F., *Christianizing the Community* (Association Press, 1917).

II. RECREATION

CHUBB, PERCIVAL, *Festivals and Play* (Harpers, 1912).

YOUNG, H. P., *Character Through Recreation* (American Sunday School Union, 1915), chap. XII; "The Girl and Her Recreations," in *Character Through Recreation*, chap. XIV; "Amusements and the Church."

WHITTAKER, R., *Laughter and Life* (American Sunday School Union, 1915).

III. YOUTH

BOWEN, L. de K., *Safeguards for City Youth* (Macmillan, 1916).

GATES, H. W., *Recreation and the Church* (University of Chicago Press, 1917).

HART, J. K., *Educational Resources of Village and Rural Community* (Macmillan, 1913).

RAUSCHENBUSCH, W., "The Rights of the Child in the Community," *Religious Education* for June, 1915.

ADDAMS, JANE, *Spirit of Youth and the City Streets* (Macmillan, 1909).

CHAPTER XIV

TRAINING WORKERS

ONE of the striking differences between the church of fifty years ago and the one of to-day lies in the extent to which the laity shares in the parish work. Formerly in very many churches the ordained clergyman was the one minister; to him was committed all the parish work, services, charities, and nearly all the teaching. In the modern church the minister is the leader who organizes all his people for service so that they become a force to carry on all the work of the parish. He ministers in the services of worship; but he depends on them to do much of the work that reaches out in other forms. In a word, the modern church conducts a group of enterprises by the services of all its people. It has become an axiom of efficiency that everyone shall have some share in the ministry of the church.*

THE VOGUE OF THE DILETTANTE

The efficiency of the modern church depends on lay service; therefore it must be evident that there can be no more efficiency in the church than there is in its workers. Where entire responsibility rested upon a few men, or on one, and where religious work was committed only to professional workers, these could be professionally trained.

---

* On lay preaching and its extent in Great Britain, see chap. IV of *The Efficient Layman*, by Henry F. Cope.

Where the work is committed to many and divided amongst the untrained the difficulties of securing efficiency are increased. We seem to have forgotten that if the church needs a trained ministry training is just as necessary when the ministers are many as when they are few, just as helpful when the work is scattered amongst the laity as when it is centred in the clergy. True, it is not possible to have the same degree and character of expertness in the work of many laymen as in that of a few professionals, but the principle is irrefutable that the degree of expertness in all establishes the measure of efficiency and of success.

It is also true when operations are democratized that the weakest and least efficient may determine the success or failure of the whole. It is not to be expected that every layman, or any, should go to a theological seminary—that would evidently be impossible to them as laymen. But it is not wise to assume that zeal to do good, or that which often passes for such zeal—assumption of religious leadership—will constitute a sufficient qualification for worth-while service. Nor is it wise to assume, as we commonly do in church work, that all lay service must be devoid of any other than native ability, that somehow God will bless work that is done by those who "mean well," even though they never move from meaning to trying. We seem to fear that lay work might no longer be of a volunteer character if the workers were really to train for it.

The modern church has discovered the layman so far as his enlistment for service is concerned, but it has not discovered fully the possibilities of training. It follows the abandoned principle of volunteer soldiering, that a warmth of devotion atones for lack of preparation. In too many

departments of American life we are fairly infected with the
vogue of the amateur.   We are almost ashamed to be caught
doing things well.

A CURRICULUM FOR SERVICE

The educational programme of the church must include
the training of its own working forces.   A church is a continuous stream of personalities; new life is ever coming up
into its force as other lives pass on from its field.   It must
be ever preparing, always training its workers for the service
they are to render.   But where has any church adopted a
programme really planned to prepare its own force?   To
what extent has it entered our consciousness when planning
the curricula of church schools that the people who were to
be taught would some day live as members and workers in
a church?   The truth is that the curriculum of instruction,
in spite of all our boasted progress in gradation and differentiation, are still planned, in many instances, on one of two
hypotheses, either that the student is about to die or that
he is expecting to live in a theological seminary.   We are
not preparing youth to live in a real society that seeks to
do God's will; there are but few attempts to train them in
the life of such a society as it would be expressed through
the church.   The majority of curricula, apparently, seek to
give the student a fairly consecutive and articulated knowledge of the Bible.   In some progressive schools the Bible
is divided according to the abilities of the child to understand it as story, literature, narrative, and history.   These
courses are determined by a "body-of-knowledge" concept:
biblical history, literature, and theology; others add courses
in later church history, and a few include instruction in

the history of modern missions and, rarely, a course on present-day social problems. The "Christian Nurture Courses" * of the Protestant Episcopal Church frankly recognize the relations of the child toward the church as a member, as one growing up in its life. But even these do not, so far, attempt in any way to train men and women, especially the young, for actual work in parishes.

A beginning has been made in the familiar teacher-training propaganda, but even the most optimistic must recognize its limitations: it prepares only for one task; the preparation is narrow; it has affected only a small number of teachers; it is not succeeding in preparing young people to begin teaching. The most serious defect, however, lies in the failure to conceive teacher training as an integral part of the whole programme of lay training. It is the duty of the church to prepare every one of its people for an intelligent and efficient share in religious usefulness. One cannot live the Christian life unless he does his full share of the work of the kingdom.

Generally speaking, at this time the church lacks consciousness of the necessity of preparing its future workers by a training which shall begin early in their lives. It has no comprehensive plans of training which look specifically to the future of children and youth in the church. It must reconsider all its curricula in the light of the kind of life and society it is seeking. It must test all courses of study by the actual experience of life in a Christian order and also by the coming experience of the students in work in churches. The church school must prepare for church service.

* First issued in 1916 and used experimentally by a selected group of schools. Published by the General Board of Religious Education, Protestant Episcopal Church, New York.

Because of the lack of a programme of training this is
what usually happens when tasks are to be assigned. At a
church meeting called for the purpose, men and women
are elected or appointed to various offices and duties. The
greater number will be persons reappointed simply because they have had experience; they have learned something of their task in the crude school of hit-and-miss. The
habitual office-holder exists not so much because he likes the
job—though that is a factor—but more because in holding
office he has had some training and the church knows it
needs trained services. The new incumbents face tasks of
which they have only the faintest conception. They must
be initiated into them through the school of bungling, un-
guided experimentation; all work must be halted or slowed
down while they are learning or perhaps paralyzed while
they make costly mistakes. We who would not think of
permitting an amateur to cut our coats, blithely commit to
wholly untrained men and women the most important enterprises for which we are responsible.

The remedy is so simple that the stating of the problem
makes its solution evident: plan and provide training, based
on the actual work of the modern church, for all youth and
young people.

CHURCH AVOCATIONAL TRAINING

If efficient workers are neither found by accident nor
born to efficiency they must be made or trained. Such training is possible only where it becomes a definite part of the
programme of the church. Here lies one of the responsibilities of the committee or board of education in the local
church, and wherever a director of religious education is

employed this is one of his duties. The committee should provide for a department of training with one or more supervisors of training who will work under the general superintendent or the director. The duties of the supervisors of training would be twofold: to see that proper and adequate courses of instruction in practical religious work are available for the preparation of all voluntary workers and to see that actual experience in developing forms of religious service is so available and attractive that workers are actually trained in and by work.

This plan calls for an extension of the present provision for the training of church-school teachers. One weakness of this work has been its artificial limitations to the work of teaching and to the immediate field of the school. Both are of prime importance, but they should be seen as integral to the whole programme of voluntary activities in the church. The special preparation of teachers will then be simply a part of the work of this department. Some of the courses now offered for teachers should be required of all who expect to do any work in religion; the especially valuable and necessary ones are those which give in simple terms an introductory study in the nature of the spiritual life and its development and in the modern methods of education.

Two divisions of instruction should be held clearly in mind: first, a series of general courses on the fundamental principles of religious work, including method and forms of organization. Second, specialized courses each dealing in greater detail with different forms or types of work. The first courses would be offered to all; they would include the present fundamental course in teacher training, together with simple courses on the organization of the church and other agencies for religious work, the history of such organizations, and the methods of various forms of parish activity.*

The second group of courses would come under two types, regular class work and series of general lectures. The *class-work* would be based upon text-book study with thorough training in actual practice under competent direction and with supervised observation and investigation. Usually only a very few courses could be carried in any one year. The teachers would be those who had had special training and experience in the fields studied. The subjects would be forms of church work, especially in relation to the general social and civic work of the parish. The courses now offered in the schools of civics and philanthropy† indicate many of the forms of training which, brought within the scope of voluntary work, would be most useful in preparation for worth-while lay service.

The *lecture courses* would be given to adults, usually, at the school period, or during the week, by leaders in different forms of social and religious work. They would be designed to stimulate to service and to more exact study. The subjects would include outstanding aspects or divisions of church work, forms of community service, immediate community problems, and the broader institutions and organizations of religious service.

PREPARING CHILDREN

It is evidently relatively easy to provide for the training of young people and adults; the more serious problem is

* Already several such courses are available, *e. g.: The Church as a Field of Service*, by C. H. Rust (American Baptist Publication Society), and *The Modern Church*, by P. A. Nordell (Scribners).

† As in New York School of Philanthropy and Chicago School of Civics.

that of preparation and training earlier in life. Since the habits of life are being determined in childhood, right social-religious habits must be formed at this time. Religious usefulness is as much a matter of attitude of mind as of aptitude or ability. Mental attitudes are taking form very early in life. The best laymen are those to whom the life of the church and its work have always been normal. Ideally the child learns the life of the church just as he learns the life of the family, by living it. But even in the family there is provision made for incidental instruction in home living. In a well-ordered family the training begins quite early in life. Similar training is needed in the life of the church. It cannot be accomplished by formal courses. But all instruction and all activities should be planned with the child's developing relations to the church in mind. In many Sunday-school lessons there are excellent, perfectly natural opportunities to develop right concepts of the church. An explanation of the meaning and work of this society which is immediately before the child's eyes is much more real and normal than attempts to reconstruct the ancient temple or the tabernacle. All such instruction should be graded according to the pupil's developing abilities to experience the life and work of the church. It should be accompanied by opportunities for active participation in that work; all graded social service should be part of churchly training.*

LABORATORY TRAINING

We cannot too strongly insist that it is altogether foolish to expect that men and women, young or old, will take seri-

* An example of the training of young children is to be found in the lessons of the *Beginner's Course* in The Completely Graded Series (Scribners).

ously or perform efficiently tasks for which they have had no preparation. We cannot too strongly insist on the right of young people, especially, to an intelligent understanding of the history, the aims, and the present methods of the church and of religious work throughout the community. But, having done all that may be done to provide courses of instruction it is wise to remember that instruction is but a small part of training. A baseball "guide" does not make a good short-stop. In fact, no boy ever thinks of looking in the guide until he has been in the game. That is true of all real training; the worth-while instruction is that which is sought because experience has revealed its necessity. Then when it is given it has meaning in reality, it stands out in the light of experience, it finds immediate, related content in the mind.

The one way to secure trained workers is to see that every one has a real opportunity to experience work. There is no appetite for training where no task is realized. This principle goes rather deeper than that which says that all instruction must be carried over into definite experience in action; it says that so far as training is concerned, the one motive which gives meaning to training rises in experience, that some effort in work precedes worth-while study. Unless training rises out of a conscious need it is likely to be only perfunctory. Its message is only a series of empty symbols unless experience gives them content. What does this involve? Simply that the directors of training will see that all along through their growing lives the boys and girls, young men and women, maintain the custom of actual participation in the service which the church does, so that training may rise out of a developing consciousness of meaning and reality in the work.

"Learning by doing" will be the guiding principle of the church in training her workers. Class instruction alone, by formal lessons, will have about the same practical results as book-lessons in swimming. But the processes by which the boys acquired facility in the old swimming-hole are much simpler than those we can use to-day in habituating young people to service in the church. Boys took to the water as to a native element; the church, too often, is foreign to them. Dashing, splashing, and performing appealed to them; we must find in church work like appeals to the strenuous and the heroic in the adolescent.

Let it be said that "learning by doing" does not mean that we acquire at once the final facilities by doing whatever they may require. We learn to walk by crawling, to do a "crawl" in the water by very rude efforts of a dog-paddle order, or by the breast stroke. The boy comes into the man's abilities as he does well and often the boy's tasks; these lead to the lad's work and this to the man's. In the church a boy's work, normally suitable for boys, is a part of the process of development through which the man's work is reached. And who knows but that the man's work is but as the infant's preparation for a larger life and its work? Avoid the blight of anticipation. It not only sets before the young impossible tasks, but to attempt them robs the future of all promise and freshness. The boy of thirteen who testifies in prayer meeting like a gray-beard and takes offices like a deacon has a desert experience before him; church-life stretches blank, with no promise of greatness yet to be achieved.

Such directed participation in work and instruction in methods does much more than secure to the church a steady stream of workers; it secures to each worker a normal, steady development in life. The church owes this training and experience to its people; it is not only a means of efficiency in the organization, it is absolutely essential to the normal development of the spiritual life of its people. It belongs in the educational programme not for the preservation of the institution, but for the purpose of meeting the necessities of growing lives. This whole life of the persons grows as it seeks to give itself away in service. It does not work in order that it may grow; it works because it is hungry for life, because it feels the passion of larger life and would give to every one that life. It counts not at all the stages of its own growth, and it measures not at all the price it pays to give life to others. While we have been looking at the mechanisms of training workers we must not allow them to obscure the movement of life. There will be no efficient workers without this passion for souls, for life, without the spirit of Him who said: "I am come that they might have life and might have it more abundantly."* This desire is the spring of all fruitful endeavor. Men find their own lives when they fling them away to give life, and the higher, finer, and more efficient the life and service they give the finer the life they find.

REFERENCES

CLARK, F. G., *Training the Church of the Future* (Funk and Wagnalls, 1902).

COPE, HENRY F., *The Efficient Layman* (American Baptist Publication Society, 1911).

SMITH, FRED. B., *A Man's Religion* (Association Press, 1913).

* John 10 : 10.

CHAPTER XV

YOUNG PEOPLE

THE problem of "the young people" is a perennial one with the church. It will cease to exist only when the church no longer has any young people. It arises from the fact that they are young people, not old people; that is to say, they are people in the making. They are the potential factors in the church. All attempts to solve the problem have been successful in the degree that they have recognized this fact and its implications. The Young People's Society movements seemed so rich in promise because they recognized some of the special needs of growing persons. They offered activities different, at least in a degree, from those for adults; they afforded a special environment; they called for activity rather than for contemplation, and they offered scope for the enthusiasms of youth.

Why, then, have the young people's societies so generally failed to realize our early high hopes? Principally because their programmes were not determined by sufficient loyalty to the fact that they were dealing with *growing* lives. They prescribed forms of worship and activity which were much like old folks' garments cut down to fit young ones. The adults had worship, prayer, and testimony meetings; it was natural to suggest: Why not let the young people have their own meetings, essentially the same, but worked out and conducted by themselves? The experiment made a strong appeal to youth because it afforded them an opportunity to have something of their own and to do some things for themselves. The first wave of enthusiasm was due to the fact that for the first time the social needs of young people were recognized by the churches. Such recognition always will secure a response in youth. But if the loyal enthusiasms are to be maintained forms of activity must be offered which grow out of the lives of youth and which express their ideals.

The Young People's Society still has a large measure of vitality where it has passed from the emphasis of wearing badges, attending conventions, and rendering testimonies. In the Christian Endeavor movement there has been a serious attempt to develop plans of normal religious activities. If the churches had more generally adopted the programmes of civic, social, and missionary activities we would have a much larger proportion of trained religious workers to-day. But the plans of the society have lacked consistency. Wisely selected activities have been paralleled by "devotional" programmes which certainly would not be normal to young people.

When these societies were first organized there were few forms of social life for the young; to-day their social programmes are likely to be crowded. Consider, as one instance, the development of social life in the modern high school. Its various clubs, societies, entertainments and activities often engross all youth's free time. Admirable as much of this social life may be, it has not found helpful relations to the work of the churches. Indeed, the tendency in many places is toward a keen sense of rivalry between churches and high schools. The churches complain that the school pre-empts all the time of young people and, also, that its social life is often harmful. The latter criticism is often just, for outside of their class-work many high schools are very like many churches, entirely without a purposeful programme for young people.

The problem persists. In spite of all that has been done it is accentuated rather than relieved; the pressure of city living, the appeals of commercialized amusements, the vogue of excitement, all make it increasingly difficult for the church to win and hold the very people who are its one hope for the next generation. What hope is there in an educational programme? It can be said at once that there is larger promise in an educational programme simply because the church has for its young people an educational purpose. Once see clearly that the church seeks first of all to develop these young lives to their fulness; acknowledge this educational process and purpose and the educational programme becomes inevitable.

AN EDUCATIONAL PROGRAMME

An educational programme for the work of the church with youth will be based upon certain quite simple considerations: What do we seek to accomplish with young people? What are their special needs and interests at this period? In what ways can the powers of their lives be applied to the programme of the church for them? The first question is answered in the already formulated aim of the church; it will be the work of the church to guide their lives into fulness, into Christlikeness, and into the habits and abilities of a Christian society.

But, simple as such a statement of purpose seems to be, it touches one of the radical causes of failure with young people. The church has not sought so much to grow them as to get them. It has been more anxious to hold them to itself than to lead them into full life. It has been thinking of their adherence rather than of their development. One still hears the lament about the young people slipping away, as though their one function was that of a limpet, to stick by the church. Of course the underlying conception is the common one that the church is an end in itself, existing for no other purpose than that people should belong to it and support it, that failure to do this is evidence of hopeless depravity and persistence therein the sole sign of grace. This notion is a part of our traditional attitude toward all institutions. But the youth is not governed by tradition. He must have a reason in values. He does not belong for the sake of belonging. He is waiting for evidence that the church has a definite purpose for him.

The church will find the first step toward the solution of the youth problem in the acceptance of the principle that all that is done is determined, not by the needs of the institution, but by some clearly seen purpose. It would make all the difference between waste and efficiency, between mere performance and accomplishment, if we should stop and ask regarding all that is done for youth: In what way is this designed to accomplish the great purpose of the church with these young people, to make their lives more Godlike, to enable them to realize a God-willed world? To hold up this standard test before all proposed schemes will save from much waste of energy. Steadily to test all plans and work in the light of that purpose will mean the gradual discovery of the importance of the next great question: What are the special needs and interests of young people?

The interests of youth are based upon their needs. The special needs of this period rise from the critical character of the years of adolescence. It is the period of conscious and deep physical changes, of readjustments in the body, and of the rise of important functions. It is the period when the will is applied not alone to single acts as they rise, but to courses of conduct, to the trend of the life. It is, above all, the time of social awakening, when lives become conscious one of another, and become conscious of the fact and the joy and force of group relationships. At this time the facts of sex differentiation become impressive and tend to strengthen social groupings. In the restless vigor of this period life's choices are being made and its habits settled. Life as an experience and a reality rises into consciousness, and what it shall mean and what it shall be is now largely determined.

What then do young people need that the church can give them?

First : Simple, personal guidance through friendship. The greatest need of every young man and every young woman is some friend, only just a little older either in years or in imagination—or both—to whom they can talk freely, who can help them over the difficult places of experience into the new facts of life. Perhaps friends of this kind may be found by planning for them, by organization; but it is doubtful if much can be accomplished to meet this need by schemes assigning older persons over younger ones. Friendships of this character come naturally by personal gravitation. And they rise out of a general condition of natural friendliness, out of normal relatedness. The youth finds friends in any group that is normal to him.

Youth grows in the soil of personality; its one outstanding appetite is for friendship. It is strongly gregarious. To be with young persons in a natural way, under normal conditions, is to do the most that can be done for them; the rest is but incidental. The church must have a real place for people who are not yet grown up and settled down. It needs an organization-consciousness below the adult stage. Where it offers a natural personal environment, a normal group of lives of young people, there the youth will find in such a group, unconsciously and without effort, those persons who meet his need for friendship, those to whom he can direct his pent-up loyalties. The real pastoral work, the personal shepherding of young people, will be done not in formal calls, but in just such ways as these, through the leadership of lives, under the tractive power of friendship, under the impulse of personal fellowship and loyalty.

Second : The sense of group relatedness. In an educational scheme, how can we provide for such relationships of youth to the church as shall develop his sense of really belonging? The church usually is not normal to youth. The boy of sixteen becomes a member; but in what sense does he belong? It is not his crowd. He feels as though he were not yet on the inside, and will not be until he can wear a frock coat with easy dignity. All the work is being done by very mature persons; they hold all offices. Except for a few other young persons, apparently quite negligible, he is an outsider.

Young people never realize membership until they have a share in work. A boy's sense of really being a part of the family grows, not out of the habit of receiving its benefits, but in the measure that he shares its duties, in the measure that he is made conscious of responsibilities. The church becomes the larger family to those who are growing out into the world's larger life in the measure that they share its work and feel the weight of its duties. This is the programme of growth for the young: to take up their work. To them the task is not irksome, for it is not a task; if it is real and worth while it is the very thing they are longing to do. They enter into life, into each day's larger area by the doors of experience and above all by the experience of the world's work.

Third : Purposeful activity. It is not work, in itself, that makes young persons grow; it is work as experience of the real, as the outreach of life in realizing itself in the larger life of the world. Youth does not grow simply because it exercises its muscles, but because it lives more largely, it takes over more of life's reality in the work and the play it experiences. Here, then, is need for caution to see that all work planned for young people is real and not factitious, that it constantly means enlarging experience of the religious life through its ways of service. Whatever the young man does must be to him convincingly valuable, consciously a part of the world's work.

THE PRINCIPLES OF ACTIVITY

Activity directed for educational purposes must have at least these five characteristics: (1) it is real; it has to the actor the sense of reality; (2) it engages the powers in some complete ways; (3) it expresses ideals already held and reaches forward into new ones; (4) it has a large measure of autonomy rising out of the will of the actor or actors; (5) it moves into group organization and direction.

Reality is a matter of experience, the consciousness in the act that it has worth of its own. Play is real to the child because he throws himself into it without analysis; it is real experience and its goals appear to him essentially worth while. There may be activity for youth which to the adult will seem to have little more basis in practical utility than play has, but to youth it will have reality and value. If we cannot always understand such values we can at least avoid the opposite error of prescribing duties which, while they have reality to us, have none to youth. These are the types of "service" usually assigned to young people by those who have allowed memory to become blurred over and imagination to die. A sympathetic imagination and a keen memory are indispensable in those who would lead youth to service.

Service which *engages the powers of the life in some complete way* means an activity into which one throws himself so as to absorb the interest and thus secure for the work an emotional backing. Such a feeling is necessary to render more easy the formation of habits, to associate pleasure with worthy work, and to develop the power of leading others into like experience. It is possible only as the tasks become absorbing, based on reality, evidently worthy and rich in possible enthusiasms. At first it may seem that tasks meeting such specifications are few indeed. But youth is susceptible; its enthusiasms are facile and responsive. It often, wisely, measures the greatness and glory of a task, not by the work itself, but by the vigor and glory one can put into it. Whatever is real and has elements of some ideality can become absorbing to youth. Watch a young man who feels the responsibility of, *e. g.*, the librarian's task in a school; watch the young officer who sees a nation's glory in his "trivial round"; watch the young woman who has the duty of leading younger girls in some simple activity. In each case the experience has an emotional backing through idealization.

Expression. Youth must be offered helpful ways of expressing ideals or it will find harmful ways, and the ideals will become swords turned back—or they will perish. The newly awakened social consciousness of youth results in an inner struggle between the self world and the social world. The experience of the past holds him to the motives of self-interest; the forward push of life would make him boldly try the experiment of altruism. Of this he dreams. When restraints are removed from conversation, when the mask of cynicism is dropped, he is an extreme altruist. If that ideal and all the faith and loyalty that go with it can be experienced in repeated conduct it will become a habit of his life. Two things are necessary now—two that go naturally together: learning and labor—that the ideal shall be clarified and strengthened both by presentation and illustration through simple teachings and by actual experience.

The loyalties of this idealistic period will fix themselves on worthy examples both in living persons and in heroes and worthies of history. Especially at the beginning of the adolescent period young people should be saturated with the lives of the truly great in all time.* All such teaching must be without moralizing, without consciousness of the

* As examples of text-books for fourteen years of age: *Heroes of the Faith* (Scribners); for girls of eighteen: *Lives Worth Living* (Univ. of Chicago Press).

purpose on the part of the learner.   Given the vision, finding himself in the eternal goodly fellowship of the great, he will seek to be worthy of them, to win his spurs, to do his work. Later he will do his own moralizing.   Whatever is learned must be lived.   Plan to keep these two not simply parallel but interwoven.

Ideal experience of the kinds suggested pushes the life out in two ways; every effort brings one to a higher plane of thinking where the air is clearer and where the further ascents, rising higher, appeal more persuasively; thus ideals develop.   Then experience reaches out into a wider fellowship, it finds wider neighborhoods.   This is absolutely necessary if the personal life is to grow, for its enriching depends on an ever-increasing variety and ever-widening number of sympathetic contacts with life through experience.   The range of activities must go out from the church into the community.   Experience must move into wider circles just as the life of the child goes from mother's arms to family circle, to school group, to community, to city, to state, to nation, and to world, nor stops there if it develop normally, but goes out to the circles that cannot be measured nor described.   We would do well to consider whether such a movement is not normal in youth's development, whether we can expect a real interest in the far until the nearer is known, whether community service does not naturally, as an experience, precede and lead to vital interest in work in other lands.

Autonomy.   Whatever youth does in the expression of the ideal life and as part of spiritual growth it must do for itself, of its own will.   Only acts rising out of a free choice can be the acts of personality.   Only through such acts can the will develop and choice be exercised toward finer discriminations. Such autonomy youth rightly craves. Here we touch the principal secret of the success of "the young people's movement" of the end of the nineteenth and beginning of the twentieth century. It was organized, largely on the principle of autonomy; young people conducted meetings, elected officers, and arranged programmes. Are we to abandon this advantage because we are confronted with problems in its exercise? The problems essential to the autonomy of this group are no more serious than those which all parents have to face in guiding their children to self-reliance, in adjusting the parent's declining authority to the youth's rising self-control. They are no more serious than those which rise in the autonomy of the women's societies and their relations to the church. We may as well recognize that it never will be possible to encourage young people to develop self-control and group-control without occasional conflicts with our own programmes and plans.

The real problem is not essentially a matter of controls; it does not rise in the fact that there is a separate society for young people, except in so far as we have regarded the matter of autonomy as a possible source of conflict and difficulty instead of seeing its tremendous and invaluable educational opportunity. If we could see, even in the experience of adjusting some organization details, of settling some difficulty, not the bother this means to us but the experience, the life training, the growth of powers it may mean to the young, we would bear with them and rejoice with them; we would refuse to sacrifice their education to our ease.

Group organization and group direction, with autonomy, are essential to youth. If the church crowd is their crowd and if their crowd has the chance to apply its energies and at the same time realize its ideals in the name and spirit of religion, it means for them all personal, spiritual growth. That group "crowd" and no other is their native spiritual habitat; they cannot be held down to the child crowd in the Sunday school and they cannot be forced up into the adult crowd. That does not mean that they will be marked off from these other two groups with impassable lines; it means that in this group they will find themselves; here they will really have the sense of belonging. Their relations to the other groups will be normal; they will help in work for children (though willingness to do this will not develop in young men until toward the end of the period of adolescence) and they will aid in work with adults, especially in community service.

PLANNING NORMAL RELATIONS

The problem of the young people persists because we have not planned our work in view of the simple needs mentioned above. We have failed to see the central importance of action in the development of the spiritual life and the importance of reality in action. We have planned for them principally three things: instruction, meetings for worship, and supervised or controlled social occasions. None of these has been immediately related to their central need of action. The instruction has not been preparatory to the work they would do nor usually even to the life which they would live. The meetings have had no vital contact with work. The social gatherings have had value precisely because they have permitted spontaneity of action and so developed in youth their own controls.

The course of instruction for youth must be determined

by the life they face and the work they can do. This is the period of interest in life's actual problems, for it is the period when they are first seen, when they are fresh and focal. The most absorbing topics to them are those revolving about conduct in its social relations. Left to themselves they spend a surprising amount of energy in discussing ethical problems, in argument over the rules of the game of life. Nor are such discussions merely academic; they rise out of experience in meeting life's difficulties. Therefore the material of instruction must be concrete, using specific problems, presenting definite "cases" and permitting freedom of discussion.* The best approaches are through the material which life presents in current events, in the great questions of the world, through presented groups of "cases" of moral conflict and questioning and through the definite situations that appear in the biographies and lives of men and women who have led their fellows.† In every case the need of action must be remembered; all instruction is with a view to its realization in action. The courses used in the school of the church should be chosen with this in mind.

Evidently a word is necessary on the relations of the young people's organization to the Sunday school; but only a very brief treatment is possible. The young people's society is simply the senior department of the church school organized for different purposes. But this separate organization of the same group leads to conflict and waste. When we see

* See a discussion of this point of view on the lessons in chaps. VIII and IX of *Efficiency in the Sunday School*, by Henry F. Cope. The method is exemplified in Johnson's *Problems of Boyhood*. See also Forbush, *Young People's Problems*.

† The limits of this work do not permit a full discussion of the curriculum for youth. This subject has been treated in *An Outline of a Sunday School Curriculum*, by G. W. Pease, 1904.

that it is the same group and, further, that the purposes
are not distinct but identical the duplication of organization becomes even less desirable. The purposes are identical
in this: the senior department is a group engaged in religious education by instruction; the young people's society
is the same group engaged in religious education by activity.
The society is simply the school engaged in giving expression
to instruction.* Why not, then, bring the two into a single
organization? Why not unify this common educational
work? Both could become the Young People's Society of
the Church School. This organization would then meet
for study as an integral part of the school and it would
meet in such other ways as it found necessary for inspiration and activities.

If it is asked what becomes of the autonomy of the young
people's organization under this scheme, the answer is that
this is to be preserved in the church school; the seniors
ought to have just that self-control already suggested for
young people. When this society meets for instruction, as
a department of the school, it places itself under the general
scheme of the school; but it should have all powers of in-
ternal government. This is desirable because at this age
youth not only demands but imperatively needs freedom
from the absolutism which is still commonly exercised over
children. If this department of the school has self-govern-
ment the very organization becomes educational in control,
in problem solution, in initiative, enterprise, and voluntary
consecration to religious purposes.

* For details of plans on this basis, see articles: W. H. Boocock, in
Religious Education, vol. V, no. 2, June, 1910, p. 177; J. A. Baber, in
Religious Education, vol. VIII, no. 5, Dec., 1913, p. 509.

SPECIAL GATHERINGS

The custom of *special meetings* for young people has a value which must not be slighted. Failure has not been due to the fact of meetings but to the fact of meaningless meetings. Meetings for the development and expression of the religious life must develop and express that life in terms consonant with youth's stage of development. This is the period when labor is prayer, when aspiration expresses itself in definite application. To be meaningful, that is, to be real, such meetings must be related to the realities of life, to concrete things largely, and certainly to the life of action and ideal service. Youth soon wearies of introspection; it becomes morbid. They have no taste for the testimony meeting that is little more than a public clinic on private spiritual ills. But they find pleasure and inspiration in gathering to plan enterprises, to stimulate one another to effort. Witness the college crowd at the rally before the field-day ! A young people's meeting should have most of its time taken in accounts of work attempted, of progress made, difficulties met, and new needs realized. It will become a conference on enterprises to be attempted. With the actualities in the foreground prayer for guidance will be natural and spontaneous and the joy of service will be worship in itself. Let all devotional forms rise out of such an atmosphere and they will maintain their reality and power. .

Social gatherings will always be maintained either under the encouragement of the church or in spite of its attitude. But the social gathering is not a device of the church to get hold of youth; it is the normal expression of youth's gregariousness. The very problems it presents—as to forms of amusement, hours, conditions—all offer just the opportunities needed for discipline. The educational value lies not in regulations imposed but through controls developed by consciousness of responsibility and by the exercise of choice and self-control. Here is one of the finest educational opportunities. Provided the ideals are made clear and vividly attractive, we must let growing lives discover and develop their powers by meeting the problems of method in social life by themselves. The objectionable becomes desirable when it is forbidden; it is usually barred when freedom of control gives the sense of social responsibility.* The social meeting is also a splendid opportunity for the exercise of altruism, when young people see that their group life is something they may share with others.

The place of young people in the church depends on our willingness to furnish opportunity for religion to express itself in terms of their present life experiences. The church becomes a normal society and a happy opportunity for them when they see in its daily programme an endeavor to make all lives full and rich and Godlike. They see the church seeking to make this world realize fully the divine plan of love and they rejoice to have full participation in such a programme. To enter into that plan is to move into the tide where life grows by its very reach after the divine ideal, its fellowship with God, and with all who are working as he works.

* This method is ably discussed in an article by Herbert W. Gates, in *Religious Education* for June, 1917.

REFERENCES

ERB, FRANK O., *Rise and Development of The Young People's Movement* (Univ. of Chicago, 1917).

FORBUSH, WM. B., *The Coming Generation* (Appleton, 1912).

MOXCEY, MARY E., *Girlhood and Character* (Abingdon, 1916).

HOBEN, ALLAN, *The Minister and the Boy* (Univ. of Chicago, 1912).

GATES, HERBERT W., articles in *Religious Education* for February, 1916, and June, 1917.

CHAPTER XVI

THE PHYSICAL

WHAT has the church to do with the programme of physical education? Has it any responsibility for teaching and habituating persons in the healthy and efficient physical life?

It must recognize as a working principle *the essential unity of the person* it seeks to educate, that he is all one, body, mind, and spirit. It must recover from the careless and misleading conception of man as a being of three natures which are temporarily in partnership. We have assumed that these different parts, each requiring a specialized ministry, can be treated in independent institutions; if the family will care for the body the school will care for the mind and the church for the spirit. Between the three sections of this layer-cake creation we have inserted separating partitions to keep the first two from contact with the last. To many it is most important that the life of thinking should not affect the life of the spirit.

But the dicta of modern science are not needed to prove that trinitarianism does not hold good in the human personality. Every-day experience reminds any observant person that the mind functions through the body and that its activities are part of the activities of the body. Thinking is translated into conduct through the muscles. Ideas are transmitted through physical action and they are received through the nerves. The clarity, exactitude, and force of every mental impression depends on the efficiency of the physical machinery for its reception. So also is the body related to the spiritual life. We are not yet disembodied spirits—though many, doubtless, would find their present religious life much simpler and less expensive if we were. The life of feeling, willing, and all that reaches beyond the physical mediates through the physical. Moral judgment depends on physical impressions and experiences. The stimuli of what is called this higher life rise through the lower levels; "faith cometh by hearing." There can be no concept of the religious life of a person cut off from all physical means of contact with others. Then, too, physical levels determine spiritual levels; the healthy body brings a full life to all its duties and its joys. Temptations are most easily met when the will is backed by normal health. Men yield when they are at the same time carrying on parallel struggles with sin and pain or fighting with a lowered resistance.

The simple fact is that when we think with care of the nature of man and the processes taking place in him it is impossible to conceive of clear-cut divisions in his personality. The man whose body you wound with a pin is the same man whose mind answers with indignation and whose spiritual life manifests itself in self-control or in passion-swept reaction. No mischievous boy has ever been able to excuse the bent pin in the deacon's pew on the ground that it was not an assault on the deacon's dignity, but only on his body, even though the deacon firmly believed in the tri-partite nature of man. Always we are dealing with a whole person. What we have called the "natures" are only the same complex called a person functioning in different ways. In his thinking he thinks as he does because of physical impressions and powers and because of religious ideals. In his working he functions physically as he does because of mental processes and spiritual concepts. And what is his religious life but the quality, color, and value of this whole life of feeling, knowing, willing, and doing?

THE CHURCH AND THE HUMAN BODY

Even these fragmentary considerations on the unity of the person with whom the church deals may be unnecessary, because, while there remains a large survival of mechanistic and traditional theory on the subject, yet in practice people are treated usually as units and few attempts are made to segregate their minds and bodies. But in religion at least we tend to divide the natures of persons according to degrees of ultimate value and degrees of immediate and functional importance. Since the spiritual life is the ultimate end we assume that we can neglect those parts which are regarded as intermediate or which are not distinctly conceived as spiritual. We no longer commonly speak of the "vile body," perhaps because it is improving and is less likely to be vile; but whenever we think of the growth of character we still assume that the body is of the least importance. In practice we act, in many respects, as though the ministry of the church was to disembodied spirits.

In general religion has held four different attitudes toward the physical: *First:* The *ascetic*, holding that the body is the foe of the spirit, a drag and a clod, a source of contamination and evil, that piety is to be promoted by the discipline of physical pain and spiritual freedom found by freedom

from this load of encumbering flesh. *Second : Separational,*
holding that the spiritual can be nurtured independent of
the body. *Third :* The *commercial,* practising the theory
that ministry to men's lower natures, that is, their bodily
needs, should be used as a means of seducing their affections
toward the church, buying allegiance by soup and sand-
wiches. *Fourth : Beneficial,* holding that it is the duty of
the church in every possible way to do as Jesus did, to go
about doing good and by the ministry to the body express
love for mankind.

But surely a deeper meaning may be found in the stories
of the healing ministry. The Saviour of men was not only
moved with compassion for the immediate hunger and
pain; there was more than profound sympathy and striking
alleviation there; just as he taught a new social order he
sought to show some of the essentials of its realization.
He knew that if men were to live in a kingdom of good-will
and joyous service they must bring the whole of themselves to it; they must be "made whole"; the members
of the society must have the elementary conditions of
righteousness, rightness within themselves, harmony in the
working machinery of life through which they were to function in the new social order. He sought an ideal society
through persons who should live ideal lives and in whom
all fitting ideals were being realized. Therefore ministry to
the body was an essential part of that pattern ministry.
And so we may seek a fifth attitude, that of *reverent faith*
which holds that the body expresses the will of God and may
be trained, disciplined, and developed to do his will.

The church will be concerned with the physical in the degree that it is seen as an essential part of the lives of persons

and therefore an essential factor in any programme for the growth of persons.   Indeed, one of the insistences of modern science is that this once-despised physical nature is fundamental in its importance; it is never negligible; it is often determinative.   It is the machinery through which all teaching must be done, through which all habits must exercise themselves, through which all knowledge must translate itself.   To all truth it gives color and force.   All knowledge becomes reality only as it finds expression through the physical act.   It is the immediate enginery of this whole creature called man.   What, then, is the ministry of the church to the physical life?

THE FIRST RESPONSIBILITY

The ministry of the church to the physical is, in many of its aspects to-day, *secondary rather than immediate*.   Only a few churches can conduct hospitals, dispensaries, and similar agencies.   But every hospital is an expression both of the past activity and the present sustaining spirit of the church.   The tendency of every efficient organization for ideal ends is to develop special agencies which independently will carry forward the actual practice of its ideals. So the church has developed very largely the ministry of healing.   The specialized forms in hospitals, sanitation, public hygiene, and the teaching of health are commonly not her immediate task, though they are her grown-up children to be fostered.

Another form of most important indirect service will be that of *the education of public opinion* to support every right effort for health and physical well-being.   This will be carried on through the advocacy of standards of physical living, through the elevation of ideals of controls of conduct, the mastery of the body and its direction in ideal service. But the fact that such service is indirect does not mean that it should be indefinite. This is not a general matter about which we can afford to feel carelessly and think loosely. It is not an indifferent question as to what the churches shall do or what the community shall do about physical well-being. We need clear thinking on health. We need definite campaigns which without losing sight of spiritual ends shall insist on the immediate importance of the physical. The church may give a worthy spiritual motive to all endeavors for community health and personal vigor.

The church will co-operate with every effort for education as to health and physical well-being. It will know what is being done through other agencies. It will co-ordinate its own plans of instruction to other community plans. It will be able to judge of the value of all such work by a thorough understanding of its principles and methods. It will carry its own share of this work. Its own courses of instruction will not lose sight of the immediate importance of the physical. It will accept its peculiar responsibility for certain aspects of instruction. Those special needs of youth which appear with the period of adolescence cannot be met apart from the motives and ideals of religion. Even the most accurate information fails without spiritual ideals and feelings of reverence. This is the most serious deficiency in what is called "sex education." The young do need the facts; the facts should be scientific; but besides the facts they need the motives and ideals.*

* See Richard C. Cabot, *What Men Live By* (Houghton, Mifflin, 1916).

INSTRUCTION ON SEX

The church cannot dodge this problem. It cannot be delegated wholly to other agencies. It will help us in considering the problem to realize that this much-discussed duty is simply a part of the whole duty of teaching and training in the laws of health. It never can be properly treated as a thing apart. It is an essential part of the whole of personal and social duty. The primary responsibility lies with the family. This is so because the training must begin before the years of schooling. Some of the highest motives for purity of living are exemplified in family life. Parents, by the continuity and informality of their relations to children, have the best and most potent opportunities for teaching.*

But few parents are prepared for these duties. They need preparation which goes beyond the facts to be taught; they need to understand the spiritual significance of the instruction and training they are to give. For the spiritual interpretation of all that has to do with the development of lives the church is responsible. Therefore the church must train parents for this task. As a part of its duty toward the religious life of the family, through its classes for parents, it will face this serious problem of the home. It will give to parents in regular courses of study and through conferences and discussions the preparation they need.

The instruction of the young in the church will be incidental, as a rule. It will come as a part of the lessons on Christian living, on social duty, on personal righteousness. Its greatest values will rise out of the influence of teachers

* See the author's *Religious Education in the Family* (Univ. of Chicago Press, 1915).

and leaders. In every church there are some men and women who, through the medium of friendship, can advise boys and girls individually. They can, under the direction or suggestion of pastor, superintendent, or director, watch for the evidences of critical needs. The real cure for the "social evil" is a society of persons who love purity passionately, who honor their fellows and love righteousness.

The church has an educational responsibility for the social conditions which permit and foster social impurity. It must teach on this subject with no uncertain sound. It must strengthen the good and denounce the evil. It must teach by its freedom from all alliance with evil. It cannot preach health if it shields those who defend vice or those who fatten on disease in any form.

DETERMINING THE SOIL OF THE SOUL

The ultimate stake of the church in the souls of men and in a spiritual society calls for an immediate aim not less than this: physical *conditions of living which make for the higher life*, a world fit for the family of God to live in. That lies back of our programmes for physical things. Clean roads, sewers, public hygiene, decent working conditions and hours, the elimination of the saloon and of every moral pest-house, all are definitely material things; but they are parts of the conditions in which the spiritual being called man lives. They constitute the soil and environment of lives. They are the silent educators. The church opposes dirt and indecency, not because she likes respectability, not because they offend her æsthetic taste, but because they function through the physical to delay and defeat her programme of a Godlike society.

Does concern for the physical tend to destroy the sense of the spiritual? Evidently the writers of the Gospels did not think so. They reveal the spiritual Jesus through his concern for humanity's immediate needs. He saw all the immediate physical in the light of the ultimate spiritual. The reality of the spiritual depends on the fulness of all the life. The man who would do God's work in this world will need all the strength he can have; he will need muscles and blood and physical habituations to carry their full load.* He must be a full man in every direction.

TRAINING FOR BOYS AND GIRLS

Has the church any responsibility for the training of the bodies of its youth and its boys and girls? Experience in the work of the church school soon brings one to face this problem. All serious plans for the welfare of youth must meet it. If young people are to grow as Christian persons they must grow in all respects; the body must be trained, educated in the spirit of Jesus, to become the servant and instrument of the will of God. Nor does this physical work minister to the body alone; it develops the whole person by the disciplines and joys of the body. It seeks to insure controls of conduct, love of noble ideals, willing service, social co-operation, and the development of the whole self on a high level.

There can be no other valid reason for any church planning for physical training. It is true that other reasons are operative, but they are sure to lead to disappointment. Many, consciously or unconsciously, argue in this way:

---

* See a stimulating article, by Dr. George J. Fisher, in *Education and National Character*, 1908, p. 99 (Religious Education Association).

boys and girls will play; they cannot be cured of it; the boys, at least, love sports and athletic contests; if we yield to their inclinations and provide the facilities for gymnastic and athletic work we may get hold of them and get them interested in the work. Anæsthetize them by athletics and then operate on them for impiety. To put it a little more precisely, churches bait the membership hook with a gymnasium. But does any fish stay on the hook of his own free will? Our modern young fish are wise and wary; if you are only baiting a hook they will nibble away at the bait for a while; they will get as far as the gymnasium but no further; in their own phrase, they will go "fifty-fifty" with you; you keep the hook and they keep the bait.

A study of the gymnasium features in churches in many States presents evidence that the most common cause of either success or failure lies in the underlying operative reason for existence. Play facilities, athletics, recreational or what you will—the big question is: Why do you have them? Unless they are instituted as essential to the real programme of the church in developing youth toward Godlikeness it were better to leave the work of amusing the young to others. Use them as a bait and the expected process is reversed; the fish pulls the rod into the stream.

This is a matter of interest to the small church as truly as to the large; both deal with youth of the same period and the same inclinations and needs; both have the same purpose and programme. The physical programme of the educational work of a church does not grow out of the congested city life alone; in fact, to-day the up-to-date city is likely to provide better facilities for physical training, at least as to the formal kind, than the open country. The problem belongs to the church everywhere because of its work of leading whole lives Godward. If the direction and development of play, the training of the body, the experience of happy social contacts and co-operation in sports and games, the development of a sound, efficient body that obeys the will and serves ideal ends are part of the making of a whole man, the church can afford neither to ignore the possibilities nor to treat the process as a device to some other end.

REFERENCES

KING, HENRY C., *Rational Living* (Macmillan, 1908).
JAMES, WILLIAM, *Talks on Psychology, Talk No.* 1 (Henry Holt, 1904).
BIGELOW, MAURICE, *Sex Education* (Macmillan, 1916). See also many papers in *Social Hygiene.*

CHAPTER XVII

THE ATHLETIC PROBLEM

s the direct responsibility of the church for pro-
e means of physical education? The answer for
rch will depend on its local conditions. As a
rinciple it may be said that it is the duty of the
to see that everywhere every provision is made
full development of the religious life and that where
r agency is capable of making any necessary special
provision the church will make it herself. This is the principle upon which all her work has been done. Her spiritual
responsibility led her to establish and conduct hospitals
when society was not ready to do the work independently.
It led her to maintain dispensaries, to conduct schools, and
to operate relief agencies. The primary responsibility is
to see that the work is done, a responsibility that can only
be discharged in some circumstances by doing it.

There is one other important consideration in favor of the
maintenance of facilities for athletic work in the church.
Inasmuch as physical training finds its highest potentiality
in the direction of the free activities of the young in play
and recreation the church as a society affords the best habitual social environment for them. Play, the idealization of
the child's experience, should be associated with the ideal
institutions. To find the play life stimulated throughout
childhood in association with the church is to acquire the
habit of playing the game of life in the church. This reason

goes very deep; it is more than a matter of associating habits. The simple fact is that the higher life and the life of play and physical development are inseparable. No clear-cut line dividing functions can be made so that we can say this belongs to the spiritual institution and that to the social or the educational. To deal with a whole life it is necessary to deal with it physically. The family offers an illuminating parallel; its all-around responsibility leads it to furnish many facilities of play and physical culture within its premises and also to exercise immediate care and guidance over all the larger fields outside.

THROUGH ORGANIZATIONS

The practical work of a church reveals the impossibility of so closely defining the field of work on the principle of specialization as to exclude provision for physical development. The work of the Boy Scouts and the Camp Fire Girls has developed in the churches; it is at home there and succeeds there best. This is because both are excellent examples of the interweaving of physical culture with moral and spiritual training. To turn these organizations out and to commit them to the schools or to other agencies because they are not limited to religious activities would be to close a thousand avenues of free access to the lives of boys and girls. In many respects they constitute the types of physical emphasis and culture which the churches can most naturally and helpfully conduct. They require no elaborate mechanisms, physical or otherwise, and no special structure or apparatus. One advantage of this is that they impose on the young no consciousness of formal and elaborate efforts on their behalf. They are built, with commendable insight

and care, on interests native to the young and they are
directed toward helpful habits. Moreover, they have the
advantage of offering a programme of greatly varied and
relatively simple forms of development.

Some who do not know the spirit of the organization suppose that the Boy Scouts is simply a military organization
giving training in "soldiering." That is not true of "The
Boys Scouts of America." It is well to know that there
are, or were, two organizations, one of which—happily now
uncovered and generally rejected—bore all the appearances
of an advertising scheme to make a new military arm.
The drill and discipline of the Scouts has no military color
aside from the uniform. Its valuable feature of first aid to
the injured is designed for all kinds of emergencies. Its
organized discipline is one of the things most needed by our
boys to-day; it would tend to make them highly valuable
in any national need. But it is not for fighting purposes;
it is scarcely possible to imagine its being so used. Before
he becomes a Scout a boy must promise as follows, in "The
Scout Oath": "On my honor I will do my best: 1. To do
my duty to God and my country and to obey the Scout law.
2. To help other people at all times. 3. To keep myself
physically strong, mentally awake, and morally straight."
The Scout law* gives twelve practicable, high ideals.

The value of the above plans for boys and girls† lies in
the manner in which they enlist their activities on many

* Given in full in *The Official Handbook* and in *The Boy Scout Movement
Applied by the Church*, Richardson and Loomis, p. 47 (Scribners, 1915).

† Full information may be secured from The Boy Scouts of America,
200 Fifth Avenue, New York; The Camp Fire Girls, 461 Fourth Avenue, New York. See, on the Scouts, *Boy Scout Movement Applied by
the Church*, N. E. Richardson and O. E. Loomis (Scribners, 1915).
See F. D. Elmer, in *Religious Education* for August, 1915, p. 364.

sides and guide them through the free play of physical powers into desirable habits and usefulness. But these two forms will not meet all needs; there will be many boys especially who are not attracted by the types of work offered in clubs, societies, and athletic organizations.

BIBLE-CLASS ATHLETIC LEAGUES

An important part of the physical work in many churches is done through the bible-class athletic leagues or the church-school leagues. In Chicago over two hundred churches are in a federated athletic organization through their schools. Such organizations exist in about one hundred and forty different cities in the United States.* They arrange match games and are supposed to supervise the standards of playing and to maintain amateur rules. The benefits reach boys and young men. The possibilities of usefulness are large. There are some dangers, however; the principal one is that the teams shall be permitted to work without proper supervision, no one caring where or when or how they play. No church should attempt this work unless it can secure the voluntary services of a man of experience in this field who will devote himself to the supervision of the teams, the standardization of their work, and the maintenance of ethical standards in play. Another danger is that there shall be no real relation of this work to the programme of the church. This does not mean athletics for the sake of the church, but the spirit and life of the church stimulating and directing this work so that the young men normally think of their life of play as a part of the life of the church.

* Report of Dr. F. J. Fisher at Federal Council of Churches, 1916, and article by Dr. Fisher describing beginnings of the Brooklyn League, in *The Aims of Religious Education*, p. 449 (1905).

Such relationships come through the constantly maintained interest of the leaders in the church and through the support which the church gives the league. There are possibilities of the development of similar work for girls.

"CHRISTIAN ASSOCIATIONS"

In many communities the more formal aspects of physical training can be best conducted by the "Christian Association." It is evidently wasteful to multiply plants for this work. If the churches could see their opportunity to accomplish their largest work unitedly the Association would become the natural agency through which many of their activities would clear. We need something wider than a church programme of physical training; we need community programmes promoted by all the churches and effected through some common representative agency such as the Y. M. C. A. or the Y. W. C. A. Of course the Associations have a work much wider than the physical, but this work they do remarkably well, and the churches would do well to use their plants and their experts. If it be objected that this would tend to disassociate men from the churches, that it runs contrary to the argument advanced above concerning the advantages of play in the church, it may be suggested that the remedy lies in identifying the associations with the churches. When a man enters a Y. M. C. A. he must feel that he enters the churches of the community in their associated capacity. It is not possible here to study in detail all the possible plans,* and we can turn only to one particular aspect of the problem.

* Valuable suggestions on provisions for the physical needs through the church are found in F. J. Milnes's *The Church and the Young Man's Game* (Doran, 1916).

THE GYMNASIUM QUESTION

There will still remain many places in which the church must make special provision for its own young people. Then the *sine qua non* is a programme and not some advertised or popular specific. Specifics are bought; programmes grow. A "physical plant" may only be a dead tree cumbering the ground. The most common delusion is that a fine gymnasium crowded with shining apparatus—dumb-bells, bars, ladders, swings, etc., etc.—will "turn the trick." And, usually, all that splendid outfit spells an expense so heavy that the church gives up almost before it begins.

Even in the formal gymnasium the present tendency is away from apparatus and toward freedom for games and play. Nearly every church can get all the best work that is now being done in physical training outside of any special building right in its back lot, on a playing-ground, or, in bad weather, in a vacant hall. Get hold of that young man or that young woman who has had some of this work and give them a chance to do the very thing they would like to do in guiding boys and girls in physical development.

But the formal training is a very small part of the educational programme in this field. The larger task is to gather up, encourage, and direct the spontaneous recreational and play life. For young people, playing together is learning to live together. At present they live more really in this area of experience than in any other. We would make that living a part of the training in living as religious persons. To this end we must know how play makes for character, we must seek to organize and direct play in healthful, happy ways, simply dropping out the debasing and developing the helpful. To accomplish such an end the church needs more than sermons on "questionable amusements" and more than a sporadic Bible-class baseball team; it needs a group of men and women who give themselves to seeing that all the boys and girls have the chance to play, have time and places, and have informal direction in forms of play that develop body and character. That involves, not so much plant and machinery as planning and people.

Some time ago there was instituted in Canada, principally through the Y. M. C. A., a series of "Standard Tests" for boys. The scheme provided for an analysis of the boy's interests and needs and for an examination into his experience, achievements, and progress in regard to such matters as physical development, mental training and abilities, general knowledge, service, and social usefulness. It provided for an examination into each boy's personal development so that his needs could be met and his rate of development determined. Similar plans are being prepared for both boys and girls in the United States.* While it is not possible to institute uniform standards and tests so that each person could be exactly graded, it is worth while to attempt to secure every possible item of exact information on the needs and the life development of growing persons. And every church ought to have, as part of its school machinery, facilities to secure just such information and to keep it corrected, as persons develop, and made a part of the data upon which work with individuals can be based.

Here, then, is a section of church service in which there has been a large amount of sporadic activity, usually lack-

* See "Standard Efficiency Tests for Boys," by E. C. Foster, in *Religious Education*, vol. XII, no. 1, p. 36, February, 1917.

ing in programme and correlation. If it can be seen that physical training is a part of the general programme of religious nurture, then might we not find a place for it as definitely as we now have a place for instruction in religion through the Sunday school or church school? It will find its place, first, through the establishment of the necessary organization for leadership. In the church there will be a group of capable persons directly charged with responsibility to see that provision is made so that the young people of the community grow in both wisdom and stature. That provision may be made in the public schools, through voluntary agencies like Christian associations, through park boards, recreation bodies, or whatever may be most efficient for this purpose. Or it may be necessary for churches to make the provision as a part of their own plants. The care of the church committee or board is simply to see that it is done, and done rightly.

REFERENCES

RICHARDSON and LOOMIS, *The Boy Scout Movement Applied by the Church* (Scribners, 1915).

EDWARDS, R. H., *Christianity and Amusements,* chap. V (Association Press, 1915).

ATKINSON, HENRY A., *The Church and the People's Play* (Pilgrim Press, 1915).

YOUNG, H. P., *Character Through Recreation* (American Sunday School Union, 1915).

CHAPTER XVIII

THE CHURCH AND THE FAMILY

THE church is not a wholly independent and autonomous social institution; its life is dependent on other groups and its future is bound up with theirs. Its relation to the life of the family is peculiarly close. It always has been so. Churches are, to a very large degree, made up of family units. No matter how highly the particular church may foster individualism, and no matter how fully society may afford freedom for each person to relate himself, as he may choose, to ecclesiastical organizations, the fact remains that families are quite likely to maintain unity in such relations. The child grows up discovering groups and rejoicing in group loyalties. Long before he has any concept of what the family "ism" means he boasts of being a "Methodist" or a "Baptist." He moves with the family group in their loyalties. The churches are dependent in no small degree on this group movement of families.

Some might suggest that identity with a church on the basis of family tradition and the influence of group loyalties was not a sufficient nor an intelligent basis. But, as a matter of fact, the operation of loyalties is one of the most important forces in the development of religious character. Church membership is much more than an outward sign of an inner intellectual assent to the doctrines of the church; it is a social expression of unity with a group, of "belonging" to those who have a common aim. The power of the church to develop lives is dependent on its power to develop loyalties.   Loyalty to an ideal group is one of the best of these.   The church is efficient in the measure that it develops the emotions and group idealisms of joy and determination, of sacrifice and effort for the things for which the group stands.   Family life to the child means so much more than food and shelter; it means a unity of thought, ideals, and feelings to which he belongs.   In this little society the principle of loyalty works with tremendous effectiveness. Now, if the impetus of the principle in the smaller group is carried over to the larger one there is a decided advantage. We may preserve the best of individualism and still have each person in the church bringing to his allegiance the added sense of the family allegiance.

STRENGTHENING THE CHURCH

The church needs the family as an aid, an extension of her occasional ministry into a continuous one.   Under the very best conditions the church reaches lives only occasionally, for a few hours of each week, while the family is in most intimate contact with them for much longer periods.   In points of primacy, continuity, normality, tradition, and immediacy the family has the advantage over every other educational agency.*   In fact, none of them can accomplish its work unless it have, in some measure, the co-operation of the family.   This is peculiarly true of the work of the church. It must depend principally on the agency which primarily influences character, which most directly and constantly affects persons as persons.

* See chaps. I to III of *Religious Education in the Family*, Cope (Univ. of Chicago Press, 1915).

The problem of the church, traced down to its ends, is almost sure to lead us to the family. All social problems at root are personal problems. The new world waits for new people. The personal agencies—those which have most to do with developing persons—are the ones to which society must look for the development of character. The church cannot carry forward her work unless she has the real and efficient co-operation of the family. Here is one instance in which the programme of the church cannot be considered apart from the power of other social organizations.

In order that her own work in religious education may go forward, what can the church do to conserve the religious values and increase the religious efficiency of the family?

TO SAVE THE FAMILY

The church may foster the essential purpose of the family, the purpose which the family has in common with the church. As an institution of the spirit its first rights are those of freedom and opportunity for the spiritual life. The church may stimulate public opinion to protect the rights of the family. First comes its right to *life*, that is, to the life that is more than toiling and eating and sleeping. The churches must co-operate to protect the family from being no more than an economic factor, a part of the present producing machinery, a mere thing that exists for things. Home conditions must be improved, for they sadly need improvement as to the simple things of space, light, comfort, and sanitation. We must elevate all low standards of conditions of living, since these are factors in determining character. But the main conflict will be against any interpretation of the family in terms of things, even of the good things of the home life, and an insistence that the family does not have its rights until its people have in it the chance to know one another, to think together, to rejoice together and grow as persons, as spirits.

We cannot stop when every man has the right to a roof and a bed and fair food; he must have more, the *leisure to live*, to find himself, to enter into the life of the family, to read and talk and play with them. The church must lead in shaping a public opinion that insists on the right of the family to be the primary institution of personality, to test it by its efficiency in developing persons. And in order that this, its chief function, may be developed, we must protect its economic rights and secure to it time and suitable conditions, all as servants of its larger aims.

Wherever there is a body of religious people organized in any way there ought to be a definite nucleus of public opinion, a group engaged in a real propaganda to secure to men *the rights of the spirit*. Such groups will insist to-day that, important as business, industry, and prosperity may be, more important than all is it that the agencies of life itself, the means by which the soul grows, shall be protected and fostered. If we would have a religious world order we must protect the right of the family to develop the life of the spirit. The work of the church is almost wholly dependent on its co-operation in this respect.

The same holds true as to the physical conditions under which many families live. It is hard to think how any one belonging to an organized group of Christians can walk by a tenement or a dwelling hovel without thinking how souls are being dwarfed in there. It is difficult to conceive of a passion for righteousness without a passionate desire to sweep earth's rookeries down, not because they abase our civic pride, but because they hinder life from growing as God would have it grow.   Perhaps we need less talk about civic programmes in our adult departments and more realization of a spiritual programme which will compel a right soil for the soul.   We must give every family a chance to have a real home.

ELEVATING POPULAR CONCEPTS

In a less definite but even more important field the church with the educational vision will render service.   Our day needs a new conscience about family life, a keenness of feeling, and a spiritual vision of its possibilities that will compel us to treat the family with reverence.   We need new ideals that will make the silly, scoffing joke about the family, the lewd story, the slighting allusion and current cynical pessimism absolutely abhorrent to us.   Before the world had a church, a Bible, or any other ordinance it had the family.   Surely it is the divine instrument not only for bringing lives into the world but also for developing them aright; and yet many who would shrink from even a pleasantry about a church ordinance will light-heartedly pass slighting jokes on family life.   We must pledge ourselves against all profanity, the profanity which profanes, makes less sacred, any good thing.   Might not members of a church pledge themselves to be guiltless of profane words and conversation about the family?

It is difficult to be brief on so important a subject!   Here are the families all about us; here are our own; and in them are the people who will be the society, the world, and the church of to-morrow.   It is but one fleeting opportunity that is ours: these children so soon grow up. But what an opportunity it is to do something to make the infinitely influential surroundings of the lives of these children such as will count for righteousness! Much is being done to make the church school potent in their lives, but that school touches them only for an hour a week while the family touches, teaches, develops them day after day, under all sorts of circumstances. What can be done that will count for more than to reach the children? And where can they be reached more effectively than through their homes?

EDUCATING HOME-MAKERS

The church will determine family life precisely as she carries on all her work: through the educational process of inspiring, persuading, and guiding the home-makers. The immediate need is better parents. We need men and women who see beyond furniture and social distinction, who can be quickened to see the family as the one agency that is dealing continuously and directly with the spiritual life of those who are just becoming the world of to-morrow, who can see that family life is the school of living in which to develop persons. The minister cannot do a greater service for the kingdom of heaven than so steadily to hold up the reality of this spiritual purpose of the family that its life becomes divine and heavenly. Let every preacher look over his record of topics and see how often he has addressed himself to this opportunity. It is of little use moulding public opinion on the place or nature of a heavenly home if we fail to stimulate it to securing the qualities of heaven in homes here.

There are still more direct ways in which the church must minister to the needs of the modern family. Under our present educational organization there exists no formal provision for training parents for the real, the fundamental, and most difficult duties of home life. Courses in domestic science prepare some few to make cookies and cakes; but who shall prepare mothers and fathers to train character? Parents know this is the real problem. The churches, together with all agencies of social life, know that not only is character the real problem but that family life has more to do with determining it than any other force that touches child life. There are several things that may be done. One of the simplest is to organize a "parents' class," to consist of parents who will follow a special course of study, usually using as a text-book one of the works dealing especially with religious education in the family.*

It can hardly be necessary to present an argument on the propriety of parents' classes in the church school. This school ought to help all in all their religious problems; certainly the modern conditions of family life present a number of these problems. The problems are very definite and concrete; they include not only questions on family worship, but of books in the home, children's lies, fighting, quarrels, all that enters into character-development.

THE HOME-MAKERS

In addition to the parents' class it will be possible in many schools to organize another which will consist of young people over eighteen years of age. This class should not have a name which indicates its special subject of study.

* The text-books suggested are: *Child Study and Child Training*, Forbush; *Religious Education in the Family*, Henry F. Cope; and *Child Nature and Child Nurture*, Edward P. St. John.

It is designed to prepare young people to take seriously the matter of marriage and the founding of home life. Experience has shown that young people looking forward to marriage are interested in the great questions of the family and its welfare. Surely they should have the opportunity to prepare for their responsibilities. The church alone can give them this preparation. It is strange that society, while recognizing the fundamental importance of the family, should make no provision to prepare men and women for its duties. The schools teach domestic science, but here is a more difficult and a more important matter. Why should not courtship, the choice of a life partner, the duties of husband and wife, the often critical matters of the family budget, the founding of family life all be studied in a class of adults in the church school? Is not such study essentially religious?

Both these classes should have teachers of wide human sympathies, persons of experience who see the religious significance of their subjects. They should be able to stimulate informal discussion of each topic or lesson. The members of the classes will be benefited more by the opportunity to talk things over than by any formal lectures or long talks no matter how able they may be. The more actual situations and problems are discussed the better. It will be found that there are no dull moments, no longings for the sound of the closing bell when actualities are under discussion. But the discussion will need guidance. The textbook should furnish outlines for each period. Topics should be stated in advance and some members should be asked to obtain information on specific points.

CONFERENCES ON FAMILY PROBLEMS

In addition to conducting classes for parents on the founding of home life, the church can render valuable service to its members and promote its own purposes by providing for *group gatherings* and conferences on the special problems that perplex parents. There are many grave questions of serious practical interest upon which all fathers and mothers, and, indeed, all who have in any way to do with the care of the young, desire help. They include such problems as family worship in the home, dealing with moral difficulties, sex instruction in the home, the recreations and amusements of the young, community conditions as they affect children, relations to the public schools, dealing with peculiar traits of temperament, studying Sunday-school lessons at home.

A *mothers' club or conference*, meeting probably on some week-day afternoon, ought to be under the adult department of the church school, belonging to the organization of the school and being fostered by it. There are many such study groups; some follow set courses of study, using text-books, and others simply arrange a series of topics for discussion. In some cases one leader has charge of all the hours over a given period. In others different leaders are secured on the ground of their special familiarity with the particular subject for each occasion. Perhaps the best plan is to get a good leader for the first series, so as to make sure of an encouraging beginning, and then to pick out a series of leaders for the next group of conferences. Here the physician, the boy specialist, the pastor, the social worker, the public-school teacher, and the librarian all may have valuable help to give.

Why not have a series of *fathers' conferences* or at least a series so arranged as to time of meeting and topics as to secure the attendance and participation of the men? We have too long assumed that the moral and religious training of the family should all be laid on the women's shoulders. The men have taken the easy part of providing the means, the women have accepted the harder one of really making the home do its work. It is not a question whether we could get the men to take over the women's work in this respect. The fact is that it needs both. Not only must there be understanding of the problem and sympathy with the methods used, but, if the work of the family is to be done in the development of religious character in children, both father and mother must do it together. It would help most men wonderfully to spend an hour once a week looking squarely at the many most difficult problems they are now inclined to dodge. We plead weariness from business when we get home; we don't want to take a fair share in bringing up Willie; if we buy his clothes his mother must take care of his character. But Willie never can be brought up without our care. He has a right to more than a share of our earnings; we owe him, as we owe our home life in its educational aspects, a fair share of ourselves.

Take one specific problem, not the largest one but one of great difficulty: what do parents know about the *sex instruction* of their children? Their faith in their children is splendid and usually well founded; children answer to such faith. But children are obtaining knowledge in this field and it is our duty to see that the knowledge is clean, helpful, positive, and constructive. How shall we impart it to them? We have a right to expect help in this matter through the church. Amongst the many other possible topics let this one have a place where it will be treated by a sane religious physician who has had to do with children and with this problem.*

Another typical problem is that of *family worship*. The difficulty lies not so much in that parents do not want to have family prayers as in that they do not know how to proceed. The old methods having passed away, they do not know how to begin with any new ones. Nor do they know where to find materials for use in family worship.† There are a few books they might read on the subject; but people do not read books very much, and books simply stare back their unchanging pages at us when we present our particular concrete problems to them. Parents who want to know how to do this or that need opportunities to discuss the actual situations that arise in their own attempts.

All are more or less familiar with the splendid accomplishments of *parent-teacher associations*. Why not have in the church frequently conferences between the parents of the children and the teachers of those children in the church school? The parents' conferences could, say once a month, resolve themselves into the parent-teacher conference of the church. Few things would do more to secure helpful cooperation between the home and the church school. The parents need to know just what the teachers in the school are trying to do with their children. Altogether the parents' conference, or home conference, meeting at regular inter-

* For a list of suitable and dependable books on this subject, see *Religious Education*, December, 1916, pp. 502, 503.

† Pamphlets of materials published by The Presbyterian Board, 1916, by The Federal Council of Churches, 1917, and The American Baptists, 1918.

vals, means the church serving the needs of both school and home by providing an open forum, under wise direction, in which most directly the actual work of training the children of our families and our school in religious character may be helpfully studied and promoted.   Mutual conference would make it possible for both home and school to co-ordinate their religious instruction.   Teachers could help parents to understand the plan of the lesson course; where graded lessons are used this would be especially helpful. Sunday-school lessons should be prepared with a consciousness of the family life of children.   One course furnishes a letter for each Sunday to be taken to the pupil's parents.* These letters familiarize the parents with the plan of the course, with the general purpose, and with the work each week.   They bring teacher and parent into co-operation. They help to create in the pupil a sense of unity between the family and the church.

REFERENCES

HODGES, GEORGE, *The Training of Children in Religion* (Appleton, 1911).

FORBUSH, WILLIAM BYRON, *Child Study and Child Training* (Scribners, 1915).

COPE, HENRY F., *Religious Education in the Family* (University of Chicago Press, 1915).

"Religious Education Association," a remarkable series of papers published in *Religious Education* in 1911.

* *The Beginners' Course*, in The Completely Graded Series (Scribners).

CHAPTER XIX

THE CHURCH AND THE PUBLIC SCHOOL

ARE these two great community institutions antagonistic? If both have educational functions, must they not find means of co-operation? Neither one can achieve its purpose without the other. The school cannot give to society competent citizens unless back of all efficiencies of living and working there are those religious motives and ideals which make work worthy and social living kindly and beneficial. The school cannot say to the church, "I have no need of thee," for in our day, when the moral life is subject to the severest strain, society needs every agency that may be able to strengthen it. Neither can the church ignore the school. Here, within its walls, the growing lives of the church spend much more time than they do with her; here they really learn to live by living. If the total influence of the school is immoral it is almost impossible for the church to turn the tide. The church most seriously needs to make an ally of every agency that touches the life of youth and, most of all, of this one which more and more tends to become the ideal and centre of the child's developing social experience.

The people of the schools need the sympathy and aid of the church, for they are working in a like cause. The school-teachers of America are the largest body of idealists in the world. One cannot imagine they are teaching for the salaries; that would be to brand them as witless folk. They are teaching because they are called to teach. They have faith in life as growth; they would rather aid persons to develop than do anything else. They know, if they are teachers at all, that they are not dealing with dull facts in books; they are dealing with vital, growing people. They are not teaching lessons; they are teaching lives. They look not to returns in graduates but to lives quickened, trained, motived to full and worthy living. They know that the purposes of education are achieved only as character is realized. Often they feel the loneliness in which they work; the business man thinks of them as making good "figurers," the home as "making Johnny behave," and the church regards them as "secular" workers. The educational aim of the church will be much more readily realized if, in their own fields, all workers for ideal ends in the community are conscious of the sympathy and aid of every other possible ally.

THE PROBLEM OF RELIGIOUS KNOWLEDGE

The church must find some scheme of correlating her work with that of the public schools so that one of the great problems of American life may be solved. We have, as yet, discovered no plan by which all children may receive a measure of instruction in religion and of direct, systematic training in religious living adequate to their life needs and to the needs of present-day social living. The family has almost everywhere abandoned every form of religious instruction and seems scarcely to be conscious of a responsibility in religious training. The church school, cramped into one short period on the day of rest, has insufficient time, only an amateur teaching force, and seldom any special equipment for the work; besides which it reaches less than one-third of the children. At least two-thirds of the children, therefore, know of religion only incidentally, usually through garbled, misleading, and perverted sources, while the other third know less about religion than about any other subject or department of knowledge.

At first thought many say, Let the public schools include religious subjects in their curricula. That seems to be a simple solution until we try it. What system of religious truth shall be taught?—yours, or mine, or that of the man whose religion we either denounce or pity? Who shall determine? They are all alike to the civil eye; the state knows no difference. Shall the question be decided by popular vote? Then there are communities where non-Christian faiths would win. Shall we leave it to the teacher? When that plan is put into practice we discover how few teachers would be acceptable to the religious scruples of parents. Apparently no plan of direct religious instruction will work in American public schools. Public instruction in religion involves ideas essentially un-American, just as it is contrary to the spirit of any free faith to depend on the power of the state for its propagation.

Not only is the public school debarred from teaching religion by the principle of freedom of conscience, and also by the fact that its workers are not trained for that purpose, it is also limited by the necessity that it should keep to its own special field of work. The community has institutions designed for religious purposes; to attempt to lay on the school the teaching of religion would be to take away from the church her peculiar duty and opportunity with regard to the young. If the day comes when the schools take care of the religious instruction of all the children it will be difficult to see any work remaining for the church with them. But that consideration is not the basic one; the function of the church specifically requires that she shall teach religion under the auspices of the institutions of religion. In order to develop lives she must furnish an environment as well as a body of knowledge. The difficulty is, how to furnish efficient instruction in view of the lack of an educational programme and an educational equipment.

THE CONDITIONS OF IMPROVEMENT

The whole situation as to religious knowledge seems to be chaotic. But one hopeful emerging sign is seen in the general public acceptance of three important considerations: first, that religion has an essential place in the education of every American child;* second, that the public school cannot furnish this essential element; and, third, that the present provision in the greater number of churches of a single weekly period of religious instruction in the "Sunday school" is wholly inadequate. The second consideration is not based alone on the legal limitations of the school in regard to teaching religion; rather it is principally founded on the inability of the school in this respect. The public school does not train its teachers in the subject of religion; it cannot formulate any commonly acceptable body of religious knowledge, and it is further limited by the fact that the purposes in mind in teaching religion are so highly personal that they cannot be achieved by the ordinary school processes. These considerations throw the burden of teaching

* *The Religious Education of an American Citizen*, F. G. Peabody, 1917.

religion on to agencies peculiarly and specifically religious. Public opinion lays this responsibility on the church.*

In view of these conditions earnest persons have for some years past been endeavoring to discover practical plans by which all children and young people should receive a larger measure of instruction in religion and to insure that this instruction should really become effectively a part of their general education. Several special forms of activity in this field are to be noted: *The Daily Vacation Bible Schools.* This is a plan of week-day instruction in religion during the summer vacation, the work being usually done in the churches.† *The distinctive experiments* of the North Dakota high schools, Colorado schools, and in New York, Gary (Indiana), and many other places all provide for work in religion by school pupils to be taken in churches or similar places outside the school building.‡

SOME PROPOSALS AND EXPERIMENTS

Legislation authorizing Bible-reading in the public schools. But the public schools are not religious institutions; they are not designed for teaching religion nor for worship. Their teachers are not selected upon any religious qualifications. The use of the Bible for teaching religion or for purposes of worship in a public school would tend to give the state power over religious doctrines and customs, interfering with

* See "How Can Religion Discharge Its Function in Public Schools," at pp. 220 ff., in *Education and National Character*, The Religious Education Association.

† See *Religious Education* for August, 1914; and *The Church Vacation School*, Harriet Chappell (Revell, 1915; 75 cents).

‡ Described in detail in free pamphlets published by The Religious Education Association, Chicago, 1916 and 1917.

freedom of conscience and taking from the church its peculiar privilege of teaching religion to the young.

Academic recognition for work done in Bible study and religion. Certain important experiments have been made in this field:

(*a*) *The North Dakota Plan.** The State high-school board authorizes a syllabus of Bible study. This may be carried on privately or in special classes outside the high school and in connection with Sunday schools taught by any pastor, priest, or other person. An examination is given at the time of the regular State examination, papers are marked by readers appointed by the State school board, and those who pass are given credit to the extent of one-half unit out of the sixteen required for high-school graduation.

(*b*) *The Colorado Plan.†* The Colorado plan was first used in connection with the State Teachers' College, Greeley, Colo. The work is under a "State Council of Religious Education." The high schools give credit for Bible study of corresponding grade, in Sunday-school classes which attain the standards of the North Central Association, to an extent not to exceed one-fourth unit for each year's work. This system requires that the teachers of such classes shall have at least an equivalent to the B.A. degree and shall have special training in the subjects which they teach, that pupils shall be eligible to membership in an accredited high school, that churches shall provide such classes with separate rooms, freedom from interruption for at least

* Originated by Prof. Vernon P. Squires of the Univ. of North Dakota; fully described in free pamphlets issued by the Religious Education Association, Chicago.

† Originated by the Rev. D. D. Forward. Described in the free pamphlet published by the Religious Education Association, Chicago.

forty-five minutes, desks for each pupil, blackboard, maps, and reference works. Credit is based upon forty recitations of forty-five minutes each for each year with a minimum of one hour of study to each lesson.

(c) *The Gary Plan.** The Gary plan provides for children of elementary and high school grades being excused from their classes for from one to six hours per week, as may be arranged, in order to attend classes in their churches. The parents elect the church and, as a rule, the churches provide special teachers. On January 31, 1918, the following churches in Gary were co-operating in maintaining three community, or neighborhood, schools, in special buildings, with employed teachers: Baptist, Episcopalian, United Presbyterian, Congregational, Methodist, Disciples, Presbyterian, English Lutheran, and Reformed Jewish. With important modifications this plan is in use in other places. It is to be noted that no school funds are used for this purpose, and no instruction is given in the public school nor are school-teachers employed. The system, however, does involve certain definite provisions on the part of the church and demands trained teachers in every church.

(d) *The Wenner Plan.*† The Wenner plan provides for excusing all students one-half day per week and allowing them to go to their respective churches for instruction. This plan proposes an adaptation of the European system to American conditions. There is a marked tendency toward modifications of this plan in the United States.

(e) *Various plans* are being tried in other places. Six

* Fully described in free pamphlets issued by the Religious Education Association, Chicago.

† See Dr. George U. Wenner's book, *Religious Education and the Public Schools*.

Episcopal churches in New York City have established week-day schools of religion which provide regular classes each day usually immediately following the adjournment of the public school. Other churches* throughout the country are trying similar plans for certain days of the week. An attempt is being made in Toledo to carry out a uniform city plan under which certain grades of the elementary school would be dismissed on certain days one period early in order to attend religious instruction in the pupils' respective churches. Some churches in New York, in Chicago, and in other parts of the country provide for regular religious instruction in a period before the opening of the public school. Experimental schools are being established, supported not only by the means of the parish but by funds from a wider field, in order that different plans may be tried and, by testing the various methods, the right one may be discovered.† At the time of writing the tendency is markedly toward classes of children meeting before and after the public-school periods each day.

(f) *The Malden School of Religious Education* is an organization planning a comprehensive programme of religious training for an entire community. Organized at Malden, Mass.,‡ in 1916, it began its work by a well-organized school of training for teachers in religion, fitting them for teaching in church schools and in week-day schools of

* In New York—April, 1917—six Episcopal, one Dutch Reformed, two Lutheran, three Methodist, one Moravian, three Presbyterian, and one Reformed Presbyterian have organized week-day instruction of school children.

† The work of a demonstration school of this kind is described in *Religious Education* for February, 1916, p. 62.

‡ Organized by Prof. Walter S. Athearn, who has published several valuable pamphlets on the work of this school.

religion.   It looks forward to complete community organization in religious education.

Work of this character necessitates a special worker, a trained teacher, in charge of all week-day instruction. Actual experience is making one other need very keenly felt, that since we have but one school of general education to each neighborhood the churches shall have as much good sense as the community and shall syndicate their teaching work in one good school of religious instruction for all children.   A community school of religion is not at all inconceivable.   It is highly desirable.   It would avoid duplication of teaching plants and would foster social unity.   A community building does not imply uniform teaching for the children of all the churches.   At first it would only provide a building with equipment for all.   It could arrange for teachers in common for churches which were able thus to agree.   It would not imply any form of community control over religious faith.*

A community building would not need to be nearly as large as that for the public school because not all the children would be in classes at the same time.   But, ultimately, as the varied possibilities of such a building were realized, it would be found best to provide facilities practically equivalent to those of the public school.   This would permit of carrying on many forms of training for all children in the community.

The significance of all these enterprises lies, first, in the

* In 1918 the churches of Gary approximate to this plan by means of two community schools.

fact that the churches are really being awakened to their responsibility for the religious instruction of children, that there is a serious attempt to secure to the child, under the conditions of American freedom of conscience, his religious heritage, and, second, that just as the public schools are beginning to recognize the propriety and value of many cultural activities outside the school building, so also the school recognizes training in religion as one of the proper elements of culture which may be given through the church or any other competent outside agency.

It is also interesting to note the manner in which the problems of religious freedom have been met in securing these adjustments. The plans mentioned above do not in any case involve the use of the school building, school equipment, school authority or school workers in their professional capacities. They are all voluntary activities in relation to which the State functions only by recognizing their values. Surely the development of so many types of plans and their successful operation under varied conditions marks an encouraging step forward in the development of education and especially in the solution of the problem of religious education under civil freedom.

Before a campaign for the week-day religious instruction of school children is begun certain principles ought to be very clear in the minds of all advocates. First, that these are plans for religious instruction *by the churches;* none contemplates either the teaching of religion in public schools or the use of school funds, school property, school authority, or school officials as such. The plans function not through the school but through the church and the family. The church provides facilities, instructors, and curricula; the family exercises its rightful authority in sending children or requiring them to take the course of study. The school, under the high-school plans, simply recognizes the academic values of the work done and, under the Gary plan, affords certain free periods in which pupils may attend church classes. Every church must stand upon an equality of opportunity. The right to give religious instruction is not derived from the schools; it is a part of the right of each church and the duty arises from the function of the church.

Second, the evident advantages of these plans cannot be realized unless we take them with sufficient seriousness to *make adequate preparation* for the work involved and to provide *to pay the bills*. This is not a new painless, payless panacea. All the plans require the provision of proper instructional quarters and equipment. This means a room, or rooms, designed for class purposes, large enough, properly —not ecclesiastically—lighted, with study desks or tables, blackboards and ventilation. Do we so seriously desire the religious instruction of our children as to make provision proportionately adequate to that which the State makes for general education or rather to that which we ourselves make through the State?

Third, adequate provision includes competent teaching. Under the high-school plans this means efficient teaching of the standard of the high-school teachers' associations. The academic standards can be attained only by professionally trained teachers. The Gary plan requires such teaching for from four to sixteen periods a week. Evidently no pastor can follow such a schedule unless he abandons nearly all other parish work. In larger churches the plan necessitates the employment of a professionally trained teacher for his or her entire time; in smaller churches it means either that several will co-operate in the greater part of the instruction or that they will secure professionally trained teachers who will give part time for pay.

The curriculum is the most serious problem in week-day instruction. At present we neither know what we should teach nor why we teach the present courses. In the Gary church schools the curriculum is the great unsolved problem. A few of the church boards are attacking it with seriousness, calling to their aid the wisdom of educators and religious leaders. But surely here is a splendid opportunity for something broader than denominational lessons. No coloring of "isms" should enter the text-books in these schools which are parallel to the public schools. Special indoctrination can be given at other times. In any case it is a pity to emphasize sectarian differences where we are endeavoring to discover methods of co-operative work. The lessons should be planned not as supplementary to the present Sunday-school courses; they should be unitary in themselves, planned as courses of instruction and training in religious living.

Further, what shall be the *relation of these schools* to the present programmes of *the Sunday schools?* Under the proposed plans, what, out of all the wide area of religious instruction—the Bible, the whole history of religion, the present work of the church, worship, daily Christian social living, and all the rest—shall belong to the Sunday school and what to the week-day school? Will the latter at length make the former unnecessary and thus leave the day more free for worship and rest? Shall we teach our distinctive doctrines or ideals in the different churches on Sundays and then be able to combine on the week-day curriculum of religion?

These by no means negligible questions are raised, not at all as insuperable obstacles, but as problems worth facing; they are suggested in the hope of stimulating all interested persons to take the present opportunities with worthy seriousness and in the confidence that such solutions will be found as will lead to high success. The opportunity is so large, the promise so alluring, that we must face all that it means. These large problems are challenging all who believe in the child for the kingdom, in the confidence of a reasonable and more adequate programme for the religious education of all our children.

REFERENCES

WOOD, CLARENCE A., *School and College Credits for Bible Study* (World Book Company, 1917).

WINCHESTER, B. S., *Religious Education in a Democracy* (Abingdon, 1917).

ATHEARN, W. S., *Religious Education and American Democracy* (Pilgrim Press, 1917).

COPE, HENRY F., *Church and School in Religious Education*, bulletin no. 4, free (American Baptist Publication Society, 1915).

RELIGIOUS EDUCATION ASSOCIATION, numerous free pamphlets, including a bibliography on this subject.

CHAPTER XX

ORGANIZING FOR RELIGIOUS EDUCATION

IT may be said that this book gathers all the work of the church together under the head of education. That is true in that it views and seeks to evaluate all church work under the educational aim and function. For if the church is loyal to her purpose of developing persons and society toward the divine ideal then she is either doing educational work or not doing her proper work at all. But there is always danger, in thinking of education in the broader, inclusive terms, that we lose ourselves in generalities and fail to deal with the specific forms of endeavor necessary to achieve the educational aim.

We know that the experience of a young man in an office, and perhaps still more in a workshop, will develop his powers, increase his abilities, and so become really a factor in his education. Yet for the sake of clear thinking we do not usually classify the factories as educational institutions. True, it would be a good plan to think more frequently of their educational responsibilities; but by educational institutions we usually mean those that have to do with organized training for life, in social groups, under directed disciplines. These definite institutions develop out of the general educational consciousness. They keep it alive and develop it. So, in the church, it is quite clear that in order efficiently to serve in religious education she must somewhere find place for specific organization in education. She must teach. With all emphasis on the real educational values of all forms of church experience there still remains the need for knowledge of the facts and ideals of religion. In order fully to discharge her educational duty the church must do the work of a school.

That instruction in religion is a real and essential part of religious education needs no argument. Knowledge functions in education to open up the race heritage, to give the facts of the world, to place in the hands the tools by which life's real work is done, and to exhibit the ideals which lead lives forward and sustain them. Therefore, the religious person needs to know the history, the literature, the facts, ideals, and principles of religion. The church is the one institution which is organized to-day to give this instruction. No other which deals with the lives of the young has either freedom or competency for the task.

THE SITUATION

A new situation has developed in regard to religious knowledge. Formerly we could count on many agencies to impart instruction in religion. The week-day school included religion in its curriculum. But gradually, irrespective of civil conditions, the general curriculum has crowded religion out. Once the family counted religious teaching as one of its regular duties. Now the family assumes that it can leave all instruction to the schools, and the schools, on their part, so far as religion is concerned, leave it all to the churches, while the churches say that for such instruction they have the "Sunday school." But let it be remembered that the Sunday school was not designed to meet such a situation as this; indeed, it has grown up without much designing of any sort so far as educational responsibility is concerned.

With the duty before us of raising a religious generation and recognizing instruction in religion as a part of that duty, it is well to face the actual situation. Only a small proportion of our child population, outside of Roman Catholic parishes, receives any regular religious instruction in the course of general education. Much less than one-half of the child population attends any kind of schools on Sunday, and even those who do attend receive less than forty minutes of instruction weekly, commonly given by persons who are not teachers, given in buildings not designed for teaching and in institutions not controlled by teaching ideals. For the forty millions of school-age children in the United States, for example, there are each week *one thousand million* (1,000,000,000) hours of general instruction and at best *eight million* (8,000,000) hours of religious instruction. In other words, in our general scheme of education, embracing both church and public schools, religion holds the proportion of eight to one thousand. Then we wonder that college students are ignorant of the Bible; rather the wonder is that they know as much as they do.

How shall this situation be met? By perfecting the present church school? That will not meet the situation. We ought to bring this institution to the fulness of its possibilities, but it must be seen as only a part of the comprehensive system of organized instruction in religion for which the churches are responsible.

THE WEAKNESS OF THE SUNDAY SCHOOL

We have leaned for a long time on the "Sunday school"; much earnest and sacrificing effort has gone into its improvement, and it has made real and noteworthy improvement in recent years. Many feel that it is still the sole solution of our problem of religious instruction. They must face certain considerations: First, one period a week can never provide sufficient time to give religion its due place in the curriculum of knowledge.* Second, religious knowledge cannot hold its due place so long as it is taught by persons who are not trained teachers; the most devoted earnestness cannot take the place of trained efficiency. Neither, on the other hand, can any degree of professional training take the place of a religious personality. But it is not unthinkable that teachers should combine both true piety and professional ability. Third, instruction in religion requires at least as good conditions of work and as suitable equipment as any other. It cannot maintain its parity with other fields of knowledge so long as the places of instruction are makeshifts designed without any reference whatever to the processes of instruction. Fourth, we do not have any generally accepted curriculum of religious knowledge. We have a fair curriculum of biblical information, but as yet only the beginnings of a course of instruction based upon the purposes of religion with the lives of those who are learning.

* Mr. George W. Pepper says, in *A Voice from the Crowd*, p. 101: "The Sunday school is, in the last analysis, an agency which attempts on one day in seven to repair the damage systematically done to the Christian theory of life during the other six. . . . If religious education is supplementary and optional the chance is very great that religion itself will soon come to be so regarded."

We are beginning to realize the need of a scientific educational basis for religious instruction. Last, we must face the question whether we ought to expect to have a real school of religion on Sundays. To the child, school is precisely what work is to the adult; it is the child's normal working discipline. It is a serious question whether we are training for the preservation of the day of rest by insisting on the child's working experience being carried over into that day. The more truly we make the church school a real school the greater the danger is in that direction.

Surely no one will leap to the conclusion that we must at once abandon all church schools. No; but we must think through the situation, in view of a real programme of the education of persons in religion, rather than in terms of existing institutions. It is not the business of religious education to save the Sunday school, but rather, in view of the fact that education deals with religious persons, to discover and secure to religion its right place in education and to provide for religious instruction.

There can hardly be any question that the church is the institution responsible for religion. Save as the family has the primary responsibility, it cannot delegate its duty to any other institution and it must be responsible for seeing that the family is faithful in this respect. For the formal instruction of the young in religion we must look to the churches. Religion must be taught in religious institutions by persons selected for their religious leadership. To give the religious instruction of the young to public agencies would mean for the church the loss of their only common vital and normal contact with young lives; they would then begin work with people when their habits and ideals were already largely formed.

A NORMAL PROGRAMME

What would constitute a normal programme for religious instruction in a church? How can the modern church discharge its responsibility for the religious training of the young?

First: By trained competent leadership. General leadership beginning in the groups or communions of churches and then working down into the individual churches. Steps are being taken in this direction. Nearly all the larger church communions have special national boards or commissions of religious education.* Gradually these are coming to include in their numbers those who can be recognized as experts in religious education, trained in education as a science and specializing in religious training.† The boards are employing such experts to direct the educational work of the churches for which they are responsible. Colleges are offering courses looking forward to such professional leadership, and the graduate schools, theological seminaries, and the like are training those who can give this leadership.‡ Secretaries of education now have a recognized place in denominational machinery, not for the promotion of college work alone, but for the development of the educational work of local churches.

Such *leadership* is needed also *within the local church.* This cannot be expected from the pastor who has been trained

* The following communions have special boards of this character: Protestant Episcopal, Baptist (Northern), Congregational, Brethren, Methodist Episcopal (Board of Sunday Schools).

† Some of the boards are requiring their salaried workers to accomplish specified professional reading each year.

‡ For particulars of the courses of training, see *Religious Education* for October, 1915.

for other tasks and who has a full schedule of other duties. He cannot give either the expert direction, which he has not himself received, nor the time necessary to secure to all the children of a parish their full right of religious instruction. It ought to be said, however, that every pastor should have sufficient training in religious education to make him fairly intelligent on this part of the work of a church. But here is a specialized field for which a new profession is being created. The "Director of Religious Education," as he is usually called, stands in relation to all the educational work of the church just as the pastor does to all its other work. He is the trained educator solely responsible for all the educational work.*

Not every church will be able to have its own director. But there would seem to be no good reason why several churches should not combine to place all their work of this kind under the direction of one expert. We have thus syndicated community enterprises in other respects, notably in our public schools. We do this to secure a recreation director in the modern village or city community. Such a plan should not and need not interfere at all with church integrity or loyalty; the same educational principles hold good in all types of churches; a director does not change his efficiencies when he goes from a Baptist to a Presbyterian church. All we need is as much common sense here as we use in other areas of life.

Second: A proper place in the organization of the church by the creation of a local body, board, or committee for the promotion and general oversight of the educational work. Just as the Methodist Episcopal Church has long required,

* See Chapter XXI, "The Direction of Religious Education."

in "The Discipline," that each church shall have its local
board of Sunday schools, so other churches meeting their
enlarged responsibilities are organizing local committees and
boards of religious education.* Amongst other things this
church board will see that the church takes the next step.

Third: Provision in the church budget for sufficient funds
to carry on the educational work. It is only necessary to
examine the budget of almost any church to realize that
churches do not yet take seriously the religious education
of the young. Compare what the community spends for
general education with what all its churches actually appropriate for religious education. Or compare the expenditures
of your own church directly for adults with its special expenditures for children.

Fourth: The provision of suitable equipment. We have
long recognized that for purposes of worship the churches
require special buildings especially designed and maintained
for that sole purpose. Why assume that the need is any
less real for the purposes of instruction? Which can the
more readily adapt itself, if adaptation be necessary, the
child or the adult? But we force the child to try to adapt
himself to the commonly more than ample provision made
for the adult. It may be questioned whether we have not
overbuilt auditoriums; certainly we have underbuilt in
schools. Remember, we are not here discussing church
schools as such, but the question of the provision necessary
to carry out the duty of the church in the religious education
of the young.†

* See Chapter XXI, " The Direction of Religious Education."
† Reference must be made again to the more detailed treatment of
the subject of buildings in the author's *Modern Sunday School* (Revell)

Of course not all churches can erect special buildings for instructional purposes. It would often be bad economy to attempt to put up a special building for a small number of children. But, again, why not do what we have done with reference to public education? Is it inconceivable that the village should have one building erected by all the religious bodies or by a group of persons with vision who would devote the building to the uses of all? Not a Sunday-school building alone, but a building designed for educational work, to be used as fully as is possible for that work. The question is no longer what sort of a building is needed to accommodate so many classes every Sunday morning, but just what physical plant is required for this larger inclusive service, for adequate provision for the religious nurture of all the children of a parish or of a community. Whatever is provided ought to be planned with at least three sets of facts in mind. These are: first, the facts as to the community, as to numbers for whom provision is to be made, including the probable increase within a period of years; second, as to types of work to be conducted, what the special conditions of the community will require, whether play and recreation work will be prominent, whether class work will be the main emphasis, the types of work which are required by the programme of the church for youth; and, third, the special requirements of educational work, conditions of lighting, heating, divisions of space, provisions for inner equipment in apparatus, blackboards, cabinets, benches, varieties of seats, arrangements for group gatherings, classes, and social occasions.

and his *Efficiency in the Sunday School* (Doran). For a careful, helpful book on the subject, see *The Sunday School Building and Its Equipment*, by H. F. Evans (Univ. of Chicago Press).

Much has been accomplished on this important detail.   A number of good buildings have been erected.* In time certain standards will be worked out. But it must be remembered that no single plan will fit all places, that each church will find special conditions requiring adaptation of standard plans and that it is always a good thing for the people of a church to study carefully their own needs and to employ trained guidance in this matter.

Fifth: A programme of instruction and training which is designed for the purpose of growing religious persons and developing them into a religious society, and which is determined as to its parts and methods by the needs and abilities of these persons at the different stages of their development. As to instruction this means a complete scheme of religious knowledge for educational purposes. Recently two forward steps have been taken as to curricula; we have begun to improve the methods of studying the Bible, particularly by grading the materials of study according to the interests and needs of growing persons, and we are now including wider ranges of religious knowledge. No church is doing educational work which does not have courses of study in the Bible graded for every stage of the life of the young. But further, it surely ought to provide orderly, graded courses of instruction by which all persons would come into their full heritage of religious knowledge applied to modern social and moral problems. Real religious instruction will not shut the student up in a house of ancient Oriental imagery, history, and literature. It will not leave the impression that the divine fatherhood resigned about 70 A. D. It will

* For a list of typical buildings and for the names of architects specializing in this field, obtain the free pamphlet issued by the Religious Education Association, Chicago.

make to-day and every day as really religious as the day of
creation or of Pentecost.   It will teach religion not alone as
a history and a literature, but as life, as the power working
in all the world for righteousness.   This wider range of material is included wherever the point of view is clearly that
of training persons for religious living.

*Sixth: Provision for the enlistment and preparation of the
working forces* for religious education.   The general propaganda in North America for teacher-training was a beginning in this direction.   The next step has been that of
offering special courses for officers.   The third step is that
which is being carried out in certain community schools of
religion,* where an attempt is made to provide training
for all forms of neighborhood service and church work in
religion.   The responsibility on each church is to see that
every worker in every field in the parish can obtain such
instruction and training as are necessary.   Teacher-training must be enlarged to include church-worker training.
The training must become an integral part of the curriculum
of the church, a part of its scheme of education, training in
the activities of the religious life.   All instruction will move
on into activity, all courses will lead forward into service;
there will be work for all and designed opportunity to acquire efficiency in the work.   We must, at present, depend
on volunteer service; but it need not and must not be an
ignorant, hindering pretense of service.†   A programme of
religious education will include, besides the courses in the
church, the support of the community institute and the aid
and encouragement of workers in securing further training

* As at Malden and at Norwood, Mass.
† See Chapter XIV on " Training Workers."

through reading courses, extension study, and summer institutes.

The programme will include all that is needed in training the religious life through its activity, through experience. The curriculum of the church will mean an interpretation of all parts of the work of a church in terms of their fitness for and their power in the processes of developing persons in righteousness.

So that the church organized for direct educational work, in order to carry out its special task of religious instruction, will have trained, competent, special leadership, designed organization, a budget for education, necessary buildings and physical equipment and a curriculum of instruction and training.

REFERENCES

ATHEARN, W. S., *The Church School* (Pilgrim Press, 1915).

COPE, HENRY F., *The Modern Sunday School and Its Present-Day Task* (Revell, 1916).

———— *Efficiency in the Sunday School* (Doran, 1912).

AMERICAN BAPTIST PUBLICATION SOCIETY, bulletin no. 2, "A Programme of Religious Education" (1912).

Education in a Local Church, Report of Commission on Religious Education, 1913.

CHAPTER XXI

THE DIRECTION OF RELIGIOUS EDUCATION

In a preceding chapter on the meaning of education it was suggested that the broader concept of education as the directed evolution of lives comes to a very much narrower focus in the study of organized methods of education. So also the inclusive, broad concept of all the work of the church focuses itself in a definite range of activities which are evidently educational. These are the explicit manifestations of the implicit ideal and spirit of education, the outward signs of the inner grace. The maintenance of the general concept will depend on the efficiency with which it is realized in specific work. The church that holds to the educational vision must visualize it concretely; under generalization it soon fades away.

Hence there will be in every church at least two specific appointments for the leadership of direct educational work. There are the committee on education and the director of religious education. This book intentionally avoids any detailed treatment of the organization and method of the church school or Sunday school; the author has already attempted to treat these subjects with some care,* but it is

* See *Efficiency in the Sunday School*, Henry F. Cope (Doran, 1912); *The Modern Sunday School and Its Present-Day Task*, Henry F. Cope (Revell, 1916); and on the history of the institution, *The Evolution of the Sunday School*, Henry F. Cope (Pilgrim Press, 1913).

necessary to show the provision which the church makes in organization for the care and oversight of the school.

THE COMMITTEE ON EDUCATION

The first in importance is the committee on education, as it is through this committee that the whole church conducts its instruction. It is the duty of this body to devise and supervise the directly educational work. We can consider here only the method by which it carries out its work in so far as it concerns the general plan of the church, leaving to other treatises the application of its plans through the school.

The committee on education will need—

First: The facts of its field. It cannot provide for needs until it knows what those needs are.* It will gather the facts as to the area for which the church is responsible, the number of persons in the field, the number of persons at different ages, and, as far as possible, the probable development of the population. Such facts are necessary in order to make proper physical provision for teaching and for group work among the young. We need the same facts here that any foresighted school board would seek before designing buildings or securing teachers.

Second: The committee will make itself conversant with *the facts of religious education* through the widest possible area. Its members will know what is being done in other places; they will gather up information from every possible source. The church should make it possible for them to

* As suggesting the field of investigation, see the author's articles on "Knowing the School's Community" and "Knowing the Pupil's Life," in *The Pilgrim Teacher*, April and May, 1917.

possess modern literature on their work. In the library will be the books and magazines dealing with the educational work of the church.

Third: In order to bring all the activities of the church in this field into orderly relation one to another the committee will make a study of *all that the church is doing in every field of endeavor.* In almost every church enough energy is being used to accomplish all its purposes if only it were properly co-ordinated and directed. In the course of time new enterprises and forms of work have been added to the programme of the church; there seemed to be sufficient reason for their beginnings, but they are being perpetuated in a traditional manner. To-day the old and the new exist side by side, and often several organizations are covering the same ground, duplicating effort and wasting energy.

Fourth: The committee will need to see its work in *graphic form.* The survey of activities should set down in tabulated form all meetings, classes, organizations, forms of service, every type of activity. First make a complete list of all; then arrange them under several tabulations, showing whether they are for worship, instruction, social life, relief, play, general recreation, financial enterprises, social service, and whatever other types may appear.

ANALYZING THE SITUATION

Next study them under a time-tabulation. Lay out a week's *time-table* by hours and set over against each hour the activity of that period. The significance of such a tabulation would be clear if it were carried over into a carefully prepared diagram or graph. There the curve would run high through certain parts of Sunday and would be quite likely to disappear on other days of the week. If, further, a special diagram is prepared showing the religious educational activities, the curve will show up on one hour only. In other words, our present plans carry the peak load on one day and at one hour. The committee would have to study whether a better distribution might not be made as to time schedules. Along with such tabulations there ought to be a study of the time schedules of boys and girls outside the church in order to plan for proper relations between the two.

Another tabulation would be under the head of *life periods*. What activities are for small children, what for boys, for girls, for young men, young women, adult men, and adult women? Some surprises may await there. There will appear many hours for adult men and women and often but one for boys and girls. To guide the committee the analysis might be carried to greater detail, showing the provision made for each year up to say twenty.

One tabulation would be on the *materials of instruction*. Granted that every Christian person should be intelligent on the following, in what way does the church provide for instruction in these subjects: the Bible, church history, missions, practical Christian living, social service, church work, Christian doctrine, religious and Christian education? Set these down in a column and over against each the organization dealing with the subject, the number of courses, teachers and classes and time. Such a study will help to make clear just why so many Christian people are totally destitute of information on subjects that are simply elementary in religious knowledge.

Organizations and fields should be the subject of another

study. How many organizations are there and what field does each seek to cover, also what is the special function of each? That usually serves to uncover a number of duplications especially in work with youth.

While we are making analytical studies we might as well include the matter of *cost*. If it is possible to arrive at anything like a fair estimate of the money cost of each activity we will have figures on which to begin the work of preparing a real budget. But we will also have one means, not the final one at all, of determining the worth of different activities.

The last tabulation will be the most difficult: to determine and analyze *results*. These may be expressed in a variety of ways, some simple, some very complex. Of course, results (1) in church membership will be included, since these are simply an indication of success in securing the enlistment of lives in the great purpose and work of the church. With all we may say of warning against the fallacy of numbers we cannot go far in the work of the church unless we secure the enlistment of persons in its programme, the uniting of individuals in its group loyalties. Then results may be seen (2) in the enlistment of the activities of persons, (3) in their developing efficiency, (4) in effects of a practical character in the community, and, most difficult of all to measure, (5) in the conduct and characters of persons. Somehow we must find out whether we are really achieving the main purposes. The processes must be all tested in the light of the product. With a programme of developing new men and women, is the church really doing this? What are the effects of Sunday-school teaching? What fruitage in lives is coming out of the young people's organizations? Are we able to trace the life effects and the social effects of the services of worship?

The organization which the committee on education directs is a larger one than the Sunday school. It is the unified, co-ordinated educational work of the whole church. The next step for the committee is to see that all the educational activities are unified in one comprehensive organization which may be known as "The School of the Church" or, more simply, "The Church School." This is the name now being widely adopted. The school which meets on Sunday is a part of the church school, so also is every other form of organized educational work, including the missionary classes, Boy Scouts, and girls' clubs.

GENERAL SUPERVISION

What are the duties of the committee on education toward this unified organization, the church school?

The committee will: (1) Serve as a church cabinet on all work in religious education. (2) Unify and co-ordinate work in Sunday school, young people's society, missionary societies, brotherhoods, and other educational agencies, providing a unified programme of religious education in the church. (3) Pass upon courses of study, standards of gradation and promotion, and departmental organization. (4) Determine requirements of teaching and pass on recommendations to the teaching staff, appointing, on the recommendation of the superintendent or director, all officers and teachers in the educational work. (5) Promote the interest of the church in religious education and secure adequate support for this work.

The committee will organize itself into appropriate subcommittees: (1) *Courses of study*, determining the material of instruction in all departments. (2) *Organizations*, correlating the different organizations under one plan of religious education. (3) *Worship*, improving the character and quality of worship. (4) *Recreation*, supervising play, athletics, excursions, and other social activities. (5) *Training*, directing the classes and "laboratory" work designed to develop efficient lay service. (6) *Service*, overseeing the plans of expressional activities for community betterment. (7) *Community Co-operation*, planning forms of co-operative work with other schools and other agencies in the community.

THE DIRECTOR

The committee plans, but direction depends also on a director. Therefore, the committee secures an individual through whom its work is applied. Such a person becomes, in fact, the superintendent of education for the church. He may be an unpaid worker, but, as the work of the church becomes more highly organized, the tendency is to secure one who is professionally trained for this task and who is wholly employed in it. If we describe in some detail the work of the professional director it will serve to do two things: to indicate the seriousness with which the educational task is now being regarded and to show what are the general aspects of the direction of educational work in a church.

A director of religious education represents a new profession; the field of service is that of the organization and direction of the educational activities of local churches.*

* There are employed in the United States and Canada, according to the records in the office of the Religious Education Association, 146 trained directors of religious education in churches. Doubtless, there

Directors differ from superintendents of Sunday schools in several respects, especially in that they are professionally trained and that they are responsible for all the educational work in a church whether in the Sunday school or in any other agency.

The rise of the directorship of religious education is a striking indication of the new earnestness and seriousness of educational purpose that has come into the modern church school or, more exactly, into the programme of the churches for the education of the young. The modern church accepts its responsibility for religious instruction, and, with graded classes and curriculum, trained teachers, and special buildings, it is seeking to place its work on a level of efficiency with the public schools.

There are several institutions offering the necessary professional training for directors of religious education. The course consists of three years' work, part of which is the same as that required for the ministry, with specialization in psychology, pedagogy, educational history, organization, and method particularly as applied to religious development. The department of directors in the Religious Education Association admits only those who have had a four-year college course or its equivalent and at least two years of special training in religious education.

Directors are not assistant pastors in the usual acceptance of that term, but are expert advisers and executive heads for all the educational work in a church or a group of churches. Usually they hold authority in their special field co-ordinate

are many not yet registered in this professional group. But the number is sufficient, in view of the fact that some have been employed for seven years, to establish this profession beyond the experimental stage.

with the authority of the pastor. Therefore they are some-times called associate pastors. In view of the fact that they have had equal professional training they are entitled to equal professional standing with the pastor.

The emphasis of the director's work is on the educational side. He may direct play, but it is with the purpose of de-veloping religious character. He may superintend moving-picture presentations, but the aim is the same. He is an educator, a specialist in the church, interpreting and guiding all activities under the educational method and ideal.

This new profession offers decided attractions to young men and women. It is an opportunity to engage directly in forms of religious work based upon modern ideals and scientific methods. It gives promise of contributing to the greatly enlarged usefulness of the churches and of solving some of their most serious problems. The work, since it deals principally with young lives, offers a field of the richest promise. Directors have an opportunity not alone to im-prove the Sunday schools but to bring together in one organization all the young people of the community.

The director plans his work and carries out his plans with the committee on education. With him they are directly responsible for the actual educational organization.

Some of the most successful work by directors is being done in relatively small places, as, for instance, at Winnetka, Illinois, where a complete programme is provided for all the boys and girls of the community through the church, which employs a director. Here the young people are busy in games, classes, and social gatherings for as many hours as they may desire to spend every day in periods outside the regular public-school work. In addition there are classes for all the different groups of adults, directed social activities, and forms of educational stimulus according to their needs.

The directors of religious education in North America have a special professional organization affiliated with the Religious Education Association.

REFERENCES

Coe, George Albert, *A Social Theory of Religious Education* (Scribners, 1917).
——— "The Administration of Religious Education in a Parish," in *Religious Education* for June, 1915.
Boocock, W. H., in *Religious Education*, vol. X, February, 1915, p. 55.
Cope, Henry F., in *Religious Education*, October, 1915, p. 444.

CHAPTER XXII

THE CHURCH AND NEW DAYS

THERE are those who tell us that the days of the church are numbered and that some new social institution must arise to take her place. This might be true; it is not inconceivable, nor are we concerned for the salvation of an institution for its own sake. If the one or the chief duty of the church is to maintain itself, doubtless it will have to go as must every fruitless tree that cumbers the ground. The place of the church in the life of to-day, and of to-morrow, and the permanency of that place, will be determined solely by the needs of society and the efficiency of the church in meeting those needs. Does our world need the church? If so, what are the special needs which the church can best meet?

The work of the church seen as a programme of religious education gives a very definite answer to that question. There are specific needs rising out of the natures of persons and out of the nature of society which to-day the church alone is capable of meeting. These needs are part of the general need for education, that is, for directed social training. Specifically, they are the needs for such training in religious living as can be given only under social conditions by a group organized socially for religious purposes. The programme of religious education in the church meets a definite social need which can be met by no other institution at present.

The adoption of an educational plan, therefore, gives to all who work in the church the consciousness of *a definite, clear, and socially necessary function.* The church ceases to be a traditional form of mechanism for the maintenance of outworn ideas and quaint customs. No man needs to apologize for her, for she is doing that which must be done and that which no other can do.

The programme of religious education gives a sense of *vitality and reality* to the work of a church. It is so clear, so simple, so explicit that one knows exactly what one is doing. It has definite plans and evident objectives. Here are all the persons of the community; they are to be trained in religious living. They are to be taught to live together as a religious society. Here, especially, are the young of the community, the future society; through religious training the church is seeking to insure that that society shall be religious in character. The special sense of vitality comes from the fact that the work of education deals directly with lives. Its outstanding duty is the development of lives. Its chief interest is as to the kind of people these boys and girls shall become. What could be more vital and what could be more valuable than this work of directing and stimulating the development of personality into the divine likeness?

DEEPER RELIGIOUS REALITY

The programme of religious education in the church gives a new depth and meaning to the *spirit of reverence.* Every true educator becomes a worshipper. To him is revealed the wonder of the laws of the growth of the spiritual life. He enters the highest realm of life and finds law reigning here, too. He gains new reverence for life itself. He learns to see it in the full measure of its values. He comes to see it in its divine aspects. He cannot help praying, in the very finest sense, whenever he has a part in the development of a life. In him there grows a sense of wonder and awe at the very work of religious education and at the fact that it lies within the range of his duties. He worships as he works. There grows all through the church this awe and wonder at life unfolding. Every spiritual sense is quickened in its presence. Religion becomes a life that is experienced in all the services and activities of such a church. All its people are working together with the infinite spirit of life, working for the increase and fulfilment of every life. They thus come to share in the divine process that ever works through all the universe. The very life of that church is in itself a religious thing. It is not a life of activity about re-ligion; *it is religion*. So that the church engaged in religious education comes herself to a fuller experience of religion.

The programme of religious education in the church gives a *new confidence and faith* as to the realization of her ideals and hopes. The work of education is based upon known laws. In an increasing degree its results are predictable. We may work, so far as the laws are known, with as great certainty in this field as in any other resting upon a scientific basis. That is simply to say that religious education seeks to discover how God works and to follow methods which are loyal to spiritual principles. So long as this is done there is no room for doubt. Here we pass into the realm of certi-tudes; we leave behind us random experiments; we discover firm ground upon which we may go forward. The religious educator does not work in the dark. He does not expect success simply because he means well. He has the light by which he may do well.   He knows why he does this or that; he knows what to expect as a consequence or result.   Whatever his doubts as to his own abilities he has none as to the results when right methods are properly used.   This is not the confidence of pride; it is the confidence of faith in law and God.

THE GROWTH OF THE CHURCH

Religious education secures the *spiritual development of the church*.   One of the distinctive marks of the Christian religion is its prophetic character.   It looks forward to determine the future.   It has been said that religions are always conservative; but Christianity is essentially constructive and regenerative.   The true church is not concerned alone with preserving the past.   It seeks only to conserve the good of the yesterdays in order to use it as a power to make the better to-morrow.   It never can be satisfied with things as they are, for it holds ideals so lofty that they are ever drawing it on to new endeavors.

Moreover, the modern church is constantly under the pressure of progress.   Realizing her social nature and responsibilities, she is consciously a part of the current social life. This life is ever changing and developing like an organism. To its developing character she must adapt her programme and according to its developing needs she must arrange her work.

But the church is an institution, and the most serious problem of every social institution is the maintenance of the prophetic mind.   How is it possible, with institutional tendencies toward conservatism, with the total gravity of institutionalism toward the *status quo*, to keep the church really in the currents of life? How can the institution conserve the force and values of the past and still, in full sympathy with the present, lead forward into the future? The educational programme furnishes the answer. The essential idea of education is development. It is always prophetic. But it uses as one of the constant forces for forward movement the experience and ideals of the past.

One condition constantly menaces every prophetic institution, that of crystallization. A fixed educational programme planned to cover the needs of many decades may be hopelessly antiquated in less than one. The adoption of any fixed programme tends to defeat the prophetic end. The work of education for the new day is possible only to those who hold a growing faith in many new days, who are unwilling to accept any one as the finality. Hospitality to new ideas and a forward-facing mind will characterize all who lead here. This will not result in a state of uncertainty. It will not invalidate programmes, for programmes are possible to vital institutions only where there is promise of progress. Religious education will train us to take with certainty the steps of to-day in the light of all the days; but it will insist that they are steps and not mere marking time. We have learned to regard education as growth; we must accustom ourselves to expecting growth and to realizing that personal growth inevitably effects social growth.

The adoption of the educational programme is the essential step of preparation to meet the needs of new days. Where growth is there change will be. The world must be ever in the making, travailing to bring forth each day a better world. If growth is going on—in other words, if God is really working in this world—we must accept the fact that the world in which our children will live will be different from our world. If we believe in growth, must we not also direct our education for purposes of growth? The more truly education is religious the more will it be a steady moving forward into the realization of ever-enlarging ideals. Surely this is religion: faith in a future that has larger values and significances than we have yet known, in a universe in which there is room to grow and to come at last to the realization of all that we have dimly felt and highly hoped, and perhaps to find that only the threshold of a larger, richer world that will include all our hopes and hungers for complete, spiritual, personal relationships.

The *method of teaching* in the modern church contributes to the habit of mind which accepts growth and development as normal. This is one of the direct benefits arising from the "historical method" of biblical study. It views the story of ancient religions as a record of progress. It discovers the steady unfolding of new ideals. Religion is seen as man's answer to the vision before him, man's stepping, often in strange ways and with many a slip and a fall, but still stepping forward into clearer light. Truth is no longer static; it is vital. The revelation grows. Thus studying the record of religion the mind acquires the habit of thinking of religious truth not as a thing but as a process. Whether in the pulpit or in the class this value must be conserved. This sense of development always at work and still working is often missed in comparing the old and the new. The teacher, in the enthusiasm of the new view, often has emphasized the external factors or has been inclined to enlarge the details of the materials discovered and to glory in these. There is a temptation to take pugnacious delight in declaring, with much show of rare courage, that there may have been fourteen Isaiahs or even none at all. In the delights of iconoclasm it is easy to forget that the shattered forms were prisons of living ideas. It is easy to classify enthusiastically the fragments while we let the living spirit escape. On the other hand, it is possible to teach the ancient Scriptures so that those who learn, with a flame of high devotion kindled in them, and with dynamic faith in life as growth, shall write the Bible of our day, to shed its light down the new days. The application of the educational method, then, tends to develop an attitude of mind which accepts growth as normal. It cultivates hospitality to new views of truth.

RELIGION A PRESENT-DAY REALITY

The programme of religious education gives to all those whose lives are developing in the church a *new sense of the present-day reality of religion*. This is due, first, to the immediate contact which modern teaching makes with the realities of experience. The curriculum is not designed as a journey of archæological exploration. It is not concerned principally with making children familiar with the remote past. It teaches life. Whatever wealth it brings from other days is for the enriching of this day. It seeks to make the great men and women of the long ago living and real to us only that our own lives, and the lives of those we teach, may be stronger and better. It gives a light to the path the pupil now treads. It makes all the difference to any child when he realizes he is not discharging a task of lessons but he is learning something about his own life and his own world.

This sense of present-day reality is further strengthened

by the direct treatment of present-day religion. We cease
to lead the child to think that the Most High has been dumb
ever since Patmos. On the contrary, if we really have faith
in life as growth, we are forced to believe that, unless man has
marked a sad recessional, God is being heard yet more clearly
with every new day. We begin to believe that the centuries
since Jesus have more for us than those that went before, not
only that God has yet more light to break forth from his
word but that he is ever speaking and we are hearing new
words. It would be an insult to infinite affection to doubt
this. No longer will children, or adults, think of these eighteen centuries gone as a long, dark way illumined only by a
great light at their beginning and by occasional torches carried aloft by certain denominational leaders.

Religion becomes native to our day. A deep need of education for the new day is such teaching on the eternal realities in every-day experience as shall make it axiomatic to
even the least child that this, our present day, is a divine era.
We shall never be fit for the future until we have faith in the
present, until the present is as sacred as the past, this land
as holy as any land, and God as present as he has ever been.

The church, accepting her work of training persons for
righteous living, gives at least as much attention to the
Christian centuries as to those which went before with their
dark beginnings, bloodshed, and dim gropings after God and
truth. It may yet give more time, issue more text-books,
and devote more attention to this neglected period of revelation, this untilled field of heroism, devotion, idealism,
faith, and progress. That will not be to slight that past;
it will be to honor its fruitage and fulfilment. That will
free us from the ghost of traditionalism, the superstitious

notion that nothing since A. D. 90 can have any religious value. To youth Savonarola will have larger values and power than Samuel and Garibaldi, or Chinese Gordon may mean much more than Joshua. What right have we to so emphatically teach that the bud was sacred and the flower is profane? God is not the god of the dead but of the living!

Moreover, this sense of present-day reality is strengthened by *facing to-day's problems*. When the church seriously attempts education for the new day she does not dodge behind the dialectics of the past to escape the duties of the present. No one even thinks of the new day without keen realization of social readjustments. This is the age of the social emphasis. To-day the individual is for the sake of the all. Almost all our modern readjustments are occasioned by this fact. The church, in her educational capacity, especially in her school, recognizes her responsibility in relation thereto. While there are many voices offering explicit teaching and definite programmes for the new social ideals, the voice of the church to-day is heard with new authority and clarity. Why this new note? Is it not because the educational emphasis has quickened a new sense of lives and of living realities? The school of the church accepts the task of training men for righteous living, right living in this world, this social order, to-day. Brought to face the problems of developing righteous lives, she comes to realize how largely social maladjustments and injustice defeat her purposes. She discovers that she must directly teach social living in the light of religious ideals, as a spiritual duty. She knows we cannot have a right world till we have righteous people, but also we cannot have people right until society is set right. No longer content with sporadic sermons, occasional lectures, and brief series of studies and discussions, she is preparing courses suited to the different grades on social duties and institutions. Why teach Hebrew institutions and neglect modern organized charities, relief problems, and methods of reform? Do not all these belong to the religious life? If we do not teach social living as a religious duty, who will?

PROPHETIC INSTRUCTION

As an agency of instruction the church does not abandon her prophetic function. Religious education is not content with the present and with the duty of preparing lives for the existing social order. It looks forward because it deals with those who must live to-morrow in a different order of society. It gathers up the light of the days that have been only to give light to the days that are to be. It reveals the race heritage of the rich past only that we may have vision and strength to push on and make the future yet richer. The religious instruction of the young must keep in mind the fact that they will live, not alone that they are living. Their world will be other than ours; we believe it will be further along the way. In the years of the Great War and the making of a new world the church does not stand aloof. The educational programmes save it from cloistered separation. When the world moves on it must lead, for its task is that of training lives for that world. Through developing lives it comes closer to the work of world-making than any other institution. As it touches the springs of conduct, the sources where character rises, it determines the character of the future.

The consciousness of this great task is constantly calling

for an examination of all curricula in the light of the question: Is this instruction planned with reference to the actual life needs of the pupil in the present and in coming years? The educational ideal establishes new standards of instruction. It requires us to look into the future with spiritual vision. It tests our faith as to whether we really can have a world of God's will. It calls on us to demonstrate that faith by preparing the young to live in such a world. It gives new reality to Isaiah's splendid vision of a redeemed land. His poetic appeals become the passion of our patriotism. It compels us to realize his vision in our world and our social order.

When she faces the future the church may do so with confidence that she holds the one solution of its problems. The new age waits for new people. All social planning will fail, all machinery of reform and regulation will be fruitless, and all attempts at building a new world by legislation will collapse unless we can touch the springs of human life in the motives, ideals, and wills of men. This is the field of religious education and the function of the church, to make a new world by and through men and women to whom all life is new because it is seen in new terms, in new relations. The church confidently goes forward forming the new world by making the new society which consists of new persons.

THE EDUCATIONAL APPEAL TO YOUTH

The programme of education gives the growing young person a new *sense of the dignity and worth of the church*. To put the matter in their own forceful terms: it becomes evident that "the church means business" with them. Young people discover values by very direct processes. They look for direct worth to themselves. They have a right to look for this in the church. They find it when it ministers directly to their needs. They appreciate it when it teaches them the way of the best life. Perhaps those who are younger are most of all impressed by the mechanisms of education. They see that the church treats them as seriously as the public school does. They come to believe in an institution that believes in them.

The programme of education provides for a *normal relation for every person* to the church. It relates itself to every life. It gives the child, at every stage of his development, a sense of really belonging. This is because the forms of its ministry are determined by the needs of his life. Thus he comes to think of the church as his church in just the same way as he thinks of his week-day school as his school. The possessive sense rises not out of any property right nor out of any power of government. It rises out of the fact that the institution is determined by the life to which it ministers.

The programme of religious education in the church offers to each one *a programme of life*. This is the case because modern education is essentially the organization of a programme of life. In childhood and youth, in young manhood and age this programme offers every one the realities of experience. It is a continuous programme. There need be no breaks. The experience offered to the boy of fifteen is just as real and full of meaning as that offered to the little child or to the adult. Therefore relations to the church are continuous. It has a place for this boy just as truly as it has for his father; it is just as natural to the boy as the father's place is to adult life. It is natural because it is his part in life. It meets the hunger of the young for activity. It offers to the youth many forms of ideal service. At every point it meets the needs of his life, for the programme is being determined with those needs in mind. At every step it indicates the duty to be done, the new steps to be taken. It guides in a life experience. Young people live in such a church. The experience of living creates a unity that is implicit. Such a church is not as one standing beside life calling a few to leave its ways and walk with her. The church, in all her work and experiences, is a way of life. The young grow up and find in her life the opportunities they always seek for wider, deeper, higher living.

Does some one say, this is an idealized picture, a prophecy born of hope and theory? The answer is to be seen in the large number of churches where the plans which have been advocated are already in operation. And further evidence of the practicability of the plans and the value of the ideals is seen in the much larger number in which efforts are being made to adopt an educational programme. Under practically every plan described, under every ideal emphasized, specific instances could have been cited where a church or often many churches were actually doing these very things. It has seemed best to omit descriptions of particular plans principally because of the diverting burden of details and also because all plans are commonly in a state of development so far as the exact particulars of method are concerned. But all those who really know the life of the churches must know that there are many now thoroughly organized on an educational basis. They must know that this is a present-day movement of tremendous vitality, that it includes every country in the world and its leaders are also the active, recognized leaders in the work of the church.

Can one doubt as to the future of such a church? It is doing the work that God has ever been doing, guiding the race into fulness of living. Its success depends not on any subtleties of plans or intricacies of mechanism but on its loyalty to the spirit of life. It moves in harmony with that eternal spirit of life that has brought our race on through all its stages of development. It is a divine institution because it is part of the divine process of progress. It is a divine institution because it is doing this supreme work of developing religious lives and religious living. This, too, is what makes it an educational institution, for what is education in its many forms but parts of the process of developing lives according to the divine laws?

And so they who work according to the divine laws, under the educational ideal in the church, see the vision of a redeemed world. They look out on a world torn, bleeding, blindly reaching out its hands in a hunger it does not understand. They know the world seeks life; its eyes must be opened to know the abiding riches of life; its feet must be guided in the ways of justice and truth; it must be trained to live the social order of the great, common, divine family. They of such a church, therefore, begin their work with lives. Their ministry is wholly to lives. By the fruitage in persons and in society they judge all their work. Such a church becomes the minister and means of life to all men. The world knows its mission is that of giving fulness of life. It stands in the world of men and by all its ways and all its work it says: "I am come that they might have life and that they might have it more abundantly."

INDEX

271

Among some papers found in the pocket-book of Prof. S. R. Cheek of Danville, Ky., was the following written by a student at the bottom of an examination paper on the Life of Paul — the last exam. Prof. Cheek we gave: "the best that I have gotten from this course is a true knowledge of God & Christ; & my association with you & your lectures alone caused me to join the church a week ago. I am simply paid for my course."
Ky. Advocate. Sat. Apr. 21, 1923.